Comprehensive And Effective
Pastoral Care

Comprehensive And Effective
Pastoral Care
A Guide for Those in Ministry

Dr. Nevalon Mitchell Jr.

Townsend Press
Nashville, TN

COMPREHENSIVE AND EFFECTIVE PASTORAL CARE:
A GUIDE FOR THOSE IN MINISTRY
Copyright © 2017 Townsend Press
(A division of the Sunday School Publishing Board, NBC, USA, Inc.)
All rights reserved.

No part of this book may be reproduced or transmitted in any form, by any means, electronic or mechanical, including photocopying, recording, or by any information storage or retrieval system without the expressed permission in writing from the publisher. Permission requests may be addressed to Townsend Press, 330 Charlotte Avenue, Nashville, Tennessee 37201–1188; or emailed to customercare@sspbnbc.com.

Scripture quotations, unless otherwise noted, are from the King James Version of the Bible.

Those marked NIV are from the Holy Bible, NEW INTERNATIONAL VERSION® Copyright © 1973, 1978, 1984, 2011 by Biblica, Inc.® Used by permission. All rights reserved worldwide.

Printed in the United States of America

26 25 24 23 22 21 20 19 18 17   –   10 9 8 7 6 5 4 3 2 1

ISBN 978-1-939225-65-8

To my loving wife,

Mrs. Wessylyne Kaye Mitchell,

who is my sweet song at midnight,

my cool breeze on a hot summer day,

and my lifelong partner.

Contents

PREFACE xi

CHAPTER 1—So What Exactly Is Pastoral Care? 1
    Pastoral Care and Emotional Support Perspectives 4
    Four Qualifications 4
    Steps to Enhance a Healthy Pastoral Visit and Ensure Success 10
    Three Simple Steps to an Encouraging Hospital Visit 11
    Helpful Hints for Pastoral Visits to Hospital Patients 12

CHAPTER 2—Coping with Terminal Illness 15
    Major End-of-life Decisions that Must Be Made by Family
    and Patient 16
    The Role of the Spiritual Caregiver and Pastoral Care Provider
    with the Family 17
    Leading the Way to the Lord 18
    What Does the Bible Say about Coping/Dealing with a
    Terminal Illness? 19

CHAPTER 3—The Response of the Church to the Spiritual Needs
of the Terminally Ill 22
    The Five Things that Terminally Ill Patients Need 23
    The Church's Response 24

CHAPTER 4—Grief Resolution 27
    Helping Others to Mourn 27
    The Grief Stages 30
    Needs of a Grieving/Bereaved Person 32

Keys for Ministering at a Time of Grief 32
Grief Avoidance Response Styles 33
The Grieving Process 35
The Effect of Grief on the Human Body 36
Pastor/Counselor Dos and Don'ts 37
Notes to Pastors or Counselors:
Helpee/Helper Sample Conversations 40
Stages of Grief Expanded 44

CHAPTER 5—PRESENTING PROBLEMS 46
Presenting Problem in the Hospital:
End-of-life/Terminal Illness 47
Presenting Problem in the Hospital or Home:
Suicide Ideation 50
Presenting Problem in the Hospital or Home:
Combination of Medical Issues 51
Presenting Problem in the Hospital and Home:
Death of Family Member or Spouse 53
Presenting Problem in the Home: Balancing the Demands
of Work, Family, and Personal Issues 54
Presenting Problem in the Home: How to Restore a Broken
Relationship after an Affair 55
Presenting Problem in the Home: Uncertainty about What
Couples Need from Each Other in a Marriage 57
Presenting Problem in the Home and Church:
Suffering from Survivor's Guilt 58
Presenting Problem in the Home or Hospital:
Post-traumatic Stress Disorder (PTSD) 59

CHAPTER 6—**BIBLE VERSES QUICK REFERENCE** 63
    Comfort for the Terminally Ill..63
    Words of Comfort and Hope for Sick and Shut-ins 67
    Comfort and Consolation 71
    After the Burial 75
    The Resurrection 77
    How to Overcome the Fear of Death 80
    Sudden or Accidental Death 81
    The Death of a Parent 81
    Death in the Prime of Life 83
    The Death of the Aged 83
    The Death of a Child 84

BIBLIOGRAPHY 86

BIOGRAPHICAL SKETCH 88

Preface

The Spirit of the Lord is upon me, because he hath anointed me to preach the gospel to the poor; he hath sent me to heal the brokenhearted, to preach deliverance to the captives, and recovering of sight to the blind, to set at liberty them that are bruised, to preach the acceptable year of the Lord. (Luke 4:18-19)

The Scripture verse is a mandate for healing, hope, and help. My purpose, goal, and intention for writing this little book is to help pastors, ministers, and religious leaders be prepared to assist and support the people of God who come to them for help.

During my twenty-plus years in the military as a senior chaplain clinician, I was confronted with thousands of situations where service men and women and their family members needed pastoral counseling and spiritual direction. This book is an attempt to offer a step-by-step guide to provide help, hope, and healing.

—NMJ

CHAPTER 1

So What Exactly Is Pastoral Care?

Take heed therefore unto yourselves, and to all the flock, over the which the Holy Ghost hath made you overseers, to feed the church of God, which he hath purchased with his own blood. (Acts 20:28)

Jesus established the foundation and substructure for a comprehensive and thorough pastoral care plan for His church. In Luke 4:18-19, Jesus gave us the mission, mandate, and map for pastoral care—comfort and counseling. Healing and helping are two of the strongest directives involved in this mission: (1) healing the broken in heart, mind, soul, and body; and (2) helping the bruised, battered, banished, and oppressed warriors find a place of rest from the challenges of life. The essence of pastoral care—comfort and counseling—is a challenge that involves the pastor and the pew, the ordained as well as laypersons.

So what exactly is pastoral care? We hear the term as it is tossed around by people who do not have a clue as to its true meaning and significance. Dr. Felicity Kelcourse, professor of pastoral care at Christian Theological Seminary, offers an exciting course entitled "The Basics of Pastoral Care and Counseling." In it she offers this definition: "Pastoral care is the art of ministry as it refers to the psychological and theological needs of a person and faith communities."[1]

Edward P. Wimberly offers yet another approach, one that is embedded in pastoral care in the black church. Here is how he describes his modus operandi from his initial books and position in 1979 and 1991 to the current 2008 edition:

> What made *African American Pastoral Care* different from the 1979 book was the emphasis on the role of the African American pastor as storyteller. In the role of storyteller, the African American pastor was to respond to the emotional, interpersonal, and spiritual needs of persons in crises, drawing on the rich indigenous cultural legacy of storytelling within the African American community. . . . *Pastoral Care in the Black Church*, however, focused more on the mobilizing role of the African American pastor, which was to draw on the rich support systems of corporate pastoral care in its sustaining and guiding functions. The second publication kept the sustaining and guiding emphases, but they were envisioned as an extension of the indigenous storytelling model. What distinguishes this third edition from the original 1979 and 1991 editions is an awareness that the world we live in as African Americans is vastly different from the world we lived in fifteen to twenty-seven years ago. The 1979 and 1991 editions were written with the assumption that the relational and culturally connected African American community was intact.[2]

Pastoral care involves shepherding the people of God by protecting the sheep or flock; tending to the needs of the flock; strengthening the weak; feeding the flock; shielding, restoring, and encouraging them as needed. There is never a greater or more demanding time to offer pastoral care than when a person is in a hospital or crisis. Is it during these times that a person needs encouragement, restoration, healing, and hope the most, or during times of uncertainty, turmoil, and unrest? It is during these life-challenging times that a simple word of comfort from the shepherd of the flock can make all the difference in the world.

Remember that there will never be a time of greater importance than your visit to the sick or dying. Whenever a person or family is in crisis the pastoral role is always magnified. Henri Nouwen addresses this need in his book entitled *The Wounded Healer* and makes it perfectly clear what the pastor's role is at that moment.[3] The pastor is the wounded healer. That is, the person who has been called upon to heal the wounds of another struggles to take care of their own wounds.

In his book *The Compassionate Visitor*, Arthur Becker states, "Pastoral care is providing compassion—being with people—just as God is 'with us' in Jesus Christ (Immanuel—Matthew 1:23)."[4] It is because of compassion that the pastor visits those who are sick or suffering, in the hopes of replacing negative emotions that accompany sickness (e.g., fear, despair, anxiety, etc.) with a sense of peace, courage, hopefulness, and reassurance. Offering insight into the importance of visible representation in pastoral care, the author of the book of Hebrews wrote, "For this reason [Jesus] had to be made like them, fully human in every way, in order that he might become a merciful and faithful high priest" (Hebrews 2:17a, NIV).

Many people are burdened and are in need of emotional, spiritual, as well as physical healing; yet they sabotage, delay, or deny the required help. Some people, like Naaman the leper (see 2 Kings 5:1-15), seek help from the wrong person. They go to the wrong place and attempt to pay the wrong price. Their quest is for the wrong reason; they seek the wrong remedy and pray for the wrong recovery during their search for a cure rather than a healing. As a result, they end up like Naaman, frustrated and frightened until they seek the Lord's face and allow Him to provide the healing they need. There are others, like the woman with the issue of blood (see Mark 5:25-36), who are secretive, silent, evasive, and refuse to let others know they are in desperate need. Many people are also like the demon-possessed man who lived among the tombs (see Mark 5:1-15) as they struggle with the stigma and shame of mental illness and the embarrassing blemish and burden it carries with it. Pastoral care and counseling offers the comfort and care these people need to overcome the infamy and shame associated with their illnesses.

Pastoral Care and Emotional Support Perspectives

Pastoral care and emotional support must be understood from different perspectives. First are the biblical requirements. Can you think of any greater privilege than to be called to be a leader in the church of Jesus Christ? The church is His body, the temple of His Spirit, His bride, His flock, His army, and His family. Can you think of any greater responsibility than leading His church? This is why God's Word has laid before us such challenging requirements for Christian leadership. The standards are rightly high, not only for the sake of the church's vitality but also for the sake of the leader's vitality.

Four Qualifications

The chief biblical texts that delineate the requirements of leaders are 1 Timothy 3:1-13; 2 Timothy 2:1-13; Titus 1:5-9; Acts 6:1-6; and Exodus 18:21-22. According to Darrell W. Johnson, the qualifications spelled out in these passages can be summarized in four words: *commitment, conviction, competency,* and *character*.

❖ **Commitment**. Are the would-be leaders clearly committed to Jesus Christ as Savior and Lord? Is there a passion to know Him in all His fullness? While different personality types express passion differently, there must be evidence of a fire inside to know and obey the Crucified and Risen One.

❖ **Conviction**. Do the would-be leaders have biblically informed convictions about who God is, who humans are, the meaning of history, the nature of the church, and especially the meaning of Jesus' death and resurrection? Are they learning what it means to be transformed by the renewal of the mind (see Romans 12:2), to "think Christian" about every dimension of their lives—money, time, sex, family, recreation? For this reason, Paul warns against being too quick to call recent converts to leadership; commitment and conviction take time to deepen.

❖ **Competency**. Do the would-be leaders know how to make their way through the Scriptures? Can they help others find their way around the sacred pages (see 2 Timothy 2:15)? Have the would-be leaders been entrusted with appropriate gifts of the Holy Spirit (see Ephesians 4:11-12; 1 Corinthians 12:12-31; Romans 12:3-8)? Do they have a working understanding of the spiritual gifts, and can they help others discern and deploy those entrusted to them? Do they have the necessary relational skills for this position? Do their relationships manifest the integrity and love of Jesus, especially in their marriage and with their children (see 2 Timothy 3:5)? The kingdom of God, after all, is about righteousness; that is, right relationship.

❖ **Character**. Are the would-be leaders taking on the character of Jesus? Someone has astutely observed, "It is not a matter of perfection, but direction." Are the potential leaders moving toward greater and greater Christ-likeness? The lists of leadership requirements are finally about character. Do they exhibit self-control, hospitality, gentleness (control of anger), a quest for holiness, temperance? Is there evidence of dying to the love of money, to manipulation, to always having it one's own way? Are they faithful to their spouse ("husband of one wife")?[5]

It should be noted that the injunction in 1 Timothy 3:4 that requires a leader to see that his children obey him with proper respect is not a demand for perfection. Even the best parents can have children that choose to disobey them (see Luke 15). Paul's concern is that those in leadership give their best energies and time to training their children. What about being "above reproach"? The point is that as leaders we should seek to be all that the Master calls us to be. It means being above condemnation as we confess and repent of our sins and failures and seek, by grace, to grow. The biblical qualifications of a leader are commitment, conviction, competency, and character. The greatest of these is character (see 1 Timothy 3:2-4).

Second, the pastoral care giver must be able to identify, understand, and promise the pastoral care components that the people in this generation need. Henri Nouwen discusses them.[6]

- ❖ **The impersonal milieu.** In our present society we are depersonalized. Often people complain of being "lost in the crowd," being "just a number," or being a cog in the vast machinery of life. This causes a feeling of lostness, disconnectedness, and insecurity. In an impersonal milieu with a fear of death and life, we often walk a tightrope between coping and loss of control. Most of the time we are able to cope, but when we are under stress we lose control. These stressors may be entrance or exit events like death, divorce, or relocation or loss of employment. When we lose control, when our coping mechanism fails, we experience anxiety, depression, phobia, burnout, and even suicidal thoughts.

❖ **The fear of death.** We often fear an impersonal death in which we are not in control, but we are swept along by the chain of events. It is this sense of helplessness that makes us cling to material things, to the cult of eternal youth, and health.

❖ **The fear of life.** Along with the fear of death is also a fear of life. Loneliness is the worst of human sufferings. Life is meaningless and endless drudgery if there is no person to relate to and to live for. Conversely, relationships with people are often too transient to depend on.

Jesus said to Simon Peter, "Feed my lambs" (John 21:15), thus starting the mandate of pastoral care. Henri Nouwen, writing in *Creative Ministry*, identified five components of pastoral care:

1. Teaching
2. Preaching
3. Individual Pastoral Care
4. Organizing
5. Celebrating[7]

To elaborate on "Individual Pastoral Care," Nouwen went on to write this: "The education of pastors so that they might hear questions and become aware of the fact that they are needed more than they realize—that thousands of people are constantly asking life's old question: What is it all about, anyhow? Why should we eat and drink, work and play, raise money and children, and fight constantly a never-ending sequence of frustrations? Or to say with sages of yore, the Yogavasistha: 'What happiness can there be in the world where everyone is born to die?'"[8] Central to the component of Individual Pastoral Care is the care of the individual: in his or her inner life and spiritual growth; in his or her interaction with the world; and in his or her coping with the stresses of life. The pastor can be involved with his parishioners by prayer, by preaching and teaching, by fellowship through the community of the saints, by visitations, and by counseling. "The paradox of the ministry indeed is that we will find the God we want to give in the lives of the people to whom we want to give Him."[9]

Third are the differences between a chaplain who provides clinical pastoral care and a pastor who provides spiritual pastoral care. Most definitions cannot do justice to pastoral care on a day-to-day basis and how chaplains fill their time. Notice the intimacy and connectedness involved with pastoral care in a hospital setting.

- Pastoral care is holding a woman while she talks on her phone to her husband's doctor and learns they have exhausted all medical resources.
- Pastoral care is listening to a nurse vent when she has had a long day.
- Pastoral care is searching the Internet for names and addresses of contacts for trauma patients.
- Pastoral care is listening to a patient tell stories about the best parts of their life.
- Pastoral care is stroking the forehead of a woman who is dying and whose family is stuck in traffic.
- Pastoral care is inviting someone to cry in your arms.
- Pastoral care is discussing the Phillies' bullpen in August in South Philly.
- Pastoral care is praying for someone who can't pray for themselves.
- Pastoral care is playing with a toddler while his parents say goodbye to their parents.
- Pastoral care is doing word puzzles with patients to make the wait more tolerable.

- Pastoral care is advocating for patients' unmet medical needs.
- Pastoral care is hearing confessions.
- Pastoral care is listening while families struggle with medical decisions.
- Pastoral care is bearing witness to people that they are loved.
- Pastoral care is journeying alongside all who come through the doors of the hospital.[10]

Fourth, the role of spirituality in a hospital or health care facility involves "compassionate care" while serving the whole person—the physical, emotional, social, and spiritual. Dr. Rachel Naomi Remen states, "Helping, fixing, and serving are ways of seeing life. When you help, you see life as weak; when you fix, you see life as broken; and when you serve, you see life as whole."[11] Fixing and helping may be the work of the ego, and service the work of the soul. In essence, a pastor offers spiritual pastoral care from his or her soul, practical care inclusive of and summarized by the tears of sorrow, sadness of life, coupled with the fears and frustrations of living life on life's terms.

> While a pastor may take on a large part of this practical care (mostly spiritual and emotional support), God desires for the pastor to equip others to also reach out in caring service (Ephesians 4:11-12). Thus pastors, chaplains, church leaders, and other Christians who use interpersonal skills to minister care are said to be providing pastoral care, which is generally given to those who are suffering, who are relatively weak or helpless, and who need some assistance in becoming stronger or comforted. Care can take on the form of listening, visiting, encouraging, consoling, counseling, lovingly correcting, praying, and other activities.[12]

Nouwen once again helps us understand the significance of what it means to become a wounded healer. This is a model of a pastor—not a professional expert but as a wounded healer—aware of the areas of pain in his or her own life. The pastoral caregiver is not being set apart from the pain of ordinary existence. "If you prick us, will we not bleed? If you tickle us, do we not laugh?" There is a mutuality here, between the caregiver and the one who is being cared for, and an acknowledgment that only those who have experienced suffering themselves can be of help to the others. This element of mutuality prevents a dynamic from occurring, suggesting that "I'm more powerful than you" and "therefore I'm better than you."

Healing can begin when the wound and the weakness are acknowledged, and the wounded healer can then go on to bring healing to others. For a deep understanding of his own pain makes it possible for him to convert his weakness into strength and to offer his own experience as a source of healing to those who are often lost in the darkness of their own misunderstood sufferings. There are two cautions inherent in this image. The first is that the caregivers, having come through suffering themselves, should not lead to a simplistic sharing of experience: "I know exactly how you feel; I've been there too; this is what helped me." The second is that those who would offer care to others can really only do so when their own wounds have healed, or, in Nouwen's words, "open wounds stink and do not heal."[13]

Since pastoral care takes on many forms and is offered in a variety of settings, what are the key elements that will provide insight, information, and education to pastors wishing to provide successful spiritual and pastoral care?

Steps to Enhance a Healthy Pastoral Visit and Ensure Success

Pastoral visitation in the home or hospital must always be rendered with an understanding that the person is in need of comfort and healing. The substance of pastoral visits can take on many forms depending on a variety of factors. The key for the informed, educated, and trained pastor is to keep in mind who you are called to serve. Bruce L. Shelly offers seven essentials that will enhance healthy pastoral visits and ensure success:

- Determine the patient's need.
- Remember to call on the patient the day before or in the early hours before surgery.
- Minister to the family in the waiting room during surgery.
- Recognize that your presence is more important than your words.
- After a brief visit, don't hesitate to take the patient's hand firmly and appropriately without causing pain.
- Remember that the seriousness of surgery has little relationship to seriousness of which the patient views the surgery.
- When you want to share a few verses of Scripture, concentrate on the selected portions of the Psalms.[14]

Three Simple Steps to an Encouraging Hospital Visit

So what should you actually do when you visit someone in the hospital? What actions will encourage and comfort the person you are visiting? Each of these steps is intentionally God-centered.

1. **Presence**. Just being there is a tremendous encouragement. Years later, the person will not remember the conversation you had. But she will remember that you were there. Being present often means that you listen. I do the least amount of talking when I visit someone in the hospital. Often the patients are so pleased to have a visitor that they talk my ear off about their

grandkids, their years of involvement at the church, and their healing progress.

2. **Passage.** Read a passage from the Bible when you visit someone in the hospital. If you want to belabor our *P* alliteration, you might even read from the Psalms. But don't stress over picking just the right passage to match their disposition or needs. If one comes to mind, that is great. Odds are that if you read a psalm, there will be something in there that will resonate with the person to whom you are reading.

3. **Prayer.** Finish with a prayer for your congregant's physical needs and spiritual needs. I ask for requests before I pray, and often get more requests for worried spouses and prodigal grandkids than for the patients themselves."[15]

Helpful Hints for Pastoral Visits to Hospital Patients

The pastoral visit must be an intentional, deliberate, determined, prayerful act of love done with the goal of providing a pastoral or spiritual service to meet a need. Emmanuel L Williams offers these very valuable words in preparation for a hospital visit and a home visit:

DON'T
- Don't be insulted by a patient's words and attitude, or register shock at a patient's appearance.
- Don't offer false optimism about a patient's recovery or participate in criticism about the doctor, hospital, or treatment.
- Don't touch equipment (even if requested by the patient), or sit on the patient's bed.
- Don't tell the patient unpleasant news, including your troubles.
- Don't whisper when talking to relatives or medical staff in the patient's room.
- Don't break hospital rules or violate confidentiality issues.

- Don't awaken a sleeping patient unless the nurse approves.
- Don't help patients get out of bed or give food or drink without the nurse's approval.
- Don't assume a comatose patient cannot hear.

DO

- Call first to determine patient availability for a visit.
- Knock before entering a room and depend on the Lord to direct your visit.
- Observe signs, notices, and precautions on the patient's door.
- If possible, sit where you can maintain comfortable eye contact with the patient.
- Be cheerful; make pleasant conversation.
- Shape the tone and substance of your conversation from cues offered by the patient.
- Listen attentively by giving the patient your undivided attention.
- Let the patient know that it is all right to talk about sensitive subjects.
- Excuse yourself when the doctor enters the room, unless requested to stay.
- Share Scripture and ask patients if they have special needs as you prepare to pray.
- Inform the Pastoral Care Department of your visit if possible.[16]

Notes

1. Felicity Kelcourse, "P-500: Basics of Pastoral Care and Counseling," course description (Indianapolis, IN: Christian Theological Seminary, Spring 2012), 1.

2. Edward Wimberly, *African American Pastoral Care,* rev. ed. (Nashville: Abingdon Press, 2010), vii.

3. Henri Nouwen, *The Wounded Healer* (New York: Image Doubleday, 1972).

4. Arthur Becker, *The Compassionate Visitor: Resources for Ministering to People Who Are Ill* (Minneapolis: Fortress Press, 1985), 25-32.

5. Darrell W. Johnson, "Biblical Requirements of Leaders," *Christianity Today* (July 2007), http://www.christianitytoday.com/pastors/2007/july-online-only/le-040329.html.

6. Nouwen, *Wounded Healer* (2010), 60-66.

7. Henri Nouwen, *Creative Ministry* (New York: Image Doubleday, 1971), 124-125.

8. Ibid., 48.

9. Ibid., 63.

10. "My Working Definition of Pastoral Care," *Journeying Alongside* (January 2012), https://journeyingalongside.wordpress.com/2012/01/20/my-working-definition-of-pastoral-care/.

11. Rachel Naomi Remen, "Helping, Fixing, Serving," Awakin.org. (May 2000), http://www.awakin.org.

12. Douglas E. Woolley, "Pastoral Care on the New Testament Epistles" (Waxahachie, TX: Harrison School of Graduate Studies, Southwestern Assemblies of God University, Summer 2009), 1.

13. Michael Ford, *Wounded Prophet* (New York: Image Doubleday, 2010).

14. Bruce L. Shelley, "7 Essentials of a Healthy Hospital Visit," *Christianity Today Leadership Journal* (August 2012), http://www.christianitytoday.com/pastors/2012/august-online-only/healthy-hospital-visit.html.

15. Eric McKiddie, "3 Simple Steps to an Encouraging Hospital Visit," *Pastoralized*, http://www.pastoralized.com/2012/07/30/3-simple-steps-to-an-encouraging-hospital-visit/.

16. Emmanuel L. Williams, "Effective Hospital Visitation," *Enrichment Journal*, http://enrichmentjournal.ag.org/200403/200403_112_hospitalvisitation.cfm (accessed October 16, 2017).

Chapter 2

Coping with Terminal Illness

When the anxious hearts say, "Where?" He doth answer, "In my care."
"Is it life or is it death?" "Wait," he whispered, "child, have faith."
"Did they need love's tenderness?" "Is there love like mine to bless?"
"Were they frightened at the last?" "No, the sting of death is past."
"Savior, tell me, where are they?" "In my keeping night and day."
"Tell us, tell us, how it stands." "None shall pluck them from my hands."
(Anonymous)

And the ransomed of the LORD *shall return, and come to Zion with songs and everlasting joy upon their heads: they shall obtain joy and gladness, and sorrow and sighing shall flee away.* (Isaiah 35:10)

Tim was a cancer patient on one of the medical units that I covered. His diagnosis was terminal, and his medical condition affected his entire family. The trauma that his family experienced was a shock to them and to him. Even worse was how the terminal situation impacted the faith of his wife, children, and friends. Trauma shakes the faith that we know and the faith we take for granted. Too many times the stress and strain of dealing with life's challenges and struggling with the slippery slopes of traumatic end-of-life issues are too much to bear. Assumptions about life and faith are put to the test at times when it is least expected. The beliefs that love is real, that there will be a tomorrow, and that we can be safe are too often shattered with the stark reality of a terminal condition that knocks us to our knees.

Where is God when we need Him the most? Why did this thing happen to me or to us? What can we do now? Where can we turn at a time when we have no strength and cannot find answers to the questions that demand immediate answers? We have been taught that religion helps us to make sense out of nonsense and that our faith will provide relief for us to the extent that we are able to reevaluate and readjust and readapt to the problems that plague us; but now our backs are up against the wall of life. This situation—this traumatic, terminal condition—has placed us with our backs up against the unmovable brick wall of life, and the uncertainty and dissociation from our known reality and social settings has us dangling with unexplained fear, apprehension, horror, and dread.

As I assumed the role of pastor and spiritual-care provider for Tim and his family, I tried to help them find ways to cope with his terminal illness. In this situation, everyone who is a believer must realize that terminal illness always disrupts the spiritual assumptions on which we stand; and if those assumptions are not accurate, the possibility of a spiritual earthquake is probable. The possibility of severe structural damage with lingering aftershocks could be felt for years to come or, in some cases, for a lifetime. My task in this project is to offer some coping skills that I have used in previous settings to help other pilgrim travelers along life's stormy highway.

Major End-of-life Decisions that Must Be Made by Family and Patient

When the diagnosis has been made that a person is terminally ill, the family and patient have some major decisions to make. For example, should palliative care or hospice care be considered? When should discussions about a living will and the types of treatment be made? All of these questions are paramount and should become one of the first decisions that the patient and family make at this critical time in their lives. The *Journal of American Medical Association* offers these important and critical definitions:

- ❖ **Palliative care** is treatment that focuses on relieving symptoms of a disease, but not to cure the disease. In palliative care the focus is on keeping the patient comfortable by treating symptoms and by using pain-killing medications.

- ❖ **Hospice care** is a type of care that is provided for the terminally ill patient. Hospice care focuses on enhancing the dying person's quality of life rather than trying to cure the terminal illness. Hospice care is usually provided in the home but can be provided in a hospital or nursing home.

- ❖ A **living will** is a document that states what limits a patient would like to have insofar as treatment received at the end of life. Many people also execute a "Durable Power of Attorney for Health Care" as well. This document states who the patient has chosen to make medical decisions for him or her. These documents are referred to as "advanced directives" because they give notice in advance of a patient's health-care wishes. The patient should give a copy of these documents to the following people: the medical doctor, select family members, and those persons whom the patient wishes to know her or his final wishes.

The Role of the Spiritual Caregiver and Pastoral Care Provider with the Family

- Seek to move the family from a place of disbelief to a place of belief and to trust in the power of God.
- Seek to move the family to a place of acceptance of the family member's unchangeable chronic condition without bitterness.

- Assist the family in making the necessary decisions and arrangements for the care of the terminally ill family member that are agreed upon by the majority of family members, and find ways to relieve unnecessary pressure and seek solutions for unresolved problems.
- Seek to address grief and unresolved grief issues before they become an ongoing problem for a family member and family system.
- Seek to move the family toward a renewal of their spiritual health and stabilize their footing as pressures, frustrations, anger, and other internal problems surface.
- Always acknowledge the stressors of the situation and the difficulty of the task at hand for the family member in charge and for the family as a whole.
- Always share your personal understanding of the patient's concerns for his or her family without breaking confidentiality. Let them know that the patient loved them and expressed that love often.
- Always be positive and share your understanding of the patient's clinical circumstances and prognosis.
- Always share your understanding of the options and offer recommendations based on clinical experiences, tailored to the particular patient's situation and real interests.
- Be spiritual and, above everything else, be prayerful and represent God.

Leading the Way to the Lord[2]
- Those that are close to death are often more receptive to spiritual things.
- Seek to be alone with the person who is dying (Mark 4:34).
- Speak directly about judgment and eternal life (Hebrews 9:27).
- Share the problem of sin in simple terms (Romans 3:23).
- State the consequences of sin (Romans 6:23).
- Specify God's solution to [our common predicament of] sin (Romans 5:8).

- Set forth the purpose of Jesus (John 3:16).
- Single out Christ as the only way to be saved (John 14:6).
- Suggest a prayer for salvation (Acts 16:31).

What Does the Bible Say about Coping/Dealing with a Terminal Illness?

Life can throw some curve balls. Getting a terminal-illness diagnoses is among the hardest-hitting news a person can receive. Know that the Lord cares and is ever-present to help His children (Psalm 46:1). Jesus sent His Holy Spirit to guide us and to comfort us. He will never leave us (see John 14:16). In this world we will have troubles (John 16:33), no matter who we are. Note these words from Thomas J. Wooten:

> Jesus told us that in this world we would have troubles (John 16:33), and absolutely no one is spared (see Romans 5:12). Yet, coping with any degree of suffering becomes easier when we understand God's overall design to redeem our fallen world. We may not be guaranteed physical health in this life, but those who trust in God are promised spiritual security for all eternity (see John 10:27-28). Nothing can touch the soul.
>
> It is good to remember that not everything bad that happens to us is a direct result of our sin. Having a terminal illness is not proof of God's judgment on an individual. Recall the time Jesus and His disciples came upon a man who had been blind since birth. They asked Jesus, "Rabbi, who sinned, this man or his parents, that he was born blind?" Jesus responded, "Neither this man nor his parents sinned. But this happened so that the work of God might be displayed in his life" (John 9:2-3). . . .

> We may never understand the reasons for our particular trials this side of eternity, but one thing is clear: for those who love God, trials work for them, not against them (see Romans 8:28). Moreover, God will give the strength to endure any trial (see Philippians 4:13). . . .
>
> Ultimately, God's will for us is to glorify Him and to grow spiritually. He wants us to trust and depend on Him. How we react to our trials, including the trial of terminal illness, reveals exactly what our faith is like. . . .
>
> The writer of Hebrews exhorts us to consider the suffering our Savior endured so that we ourselves do not grow weary and lose heart in our own trials. It was "for the joy set before Him" that Christ was able to endure the suffering of the cross. This joy, for Christ, was obeying His Father's will (see Psalm 40:8); reconciling His Father with His creation; and being exalted to the right hand of the throne of God. Likewise, our own trials can be made more bearable when we consider the joy set before us. Our joy may come in understanding that it is through testing that God transforms us into the likeness of His Son (see Job 23:10; Romans 8:29). What we see as pain and discomfort and uncertainty, our sovereign Father (who ordains or allows every event during our time on earth) sees as transformation.
>
> Our suffering is never meaningless. God uses suffering to change us, to minister to others, and ultimately to bring glory to His name.[3]

To those who have been diagnosed with a terminal illness, as Wooten advises and I concur, make sure that you are a true child of God, having trusted Jesus as your Savior (see Romans 10:9-10). Make sure your will is completed and other important arrangements have been made. Use the remaining time God gives you to grow spiritually and minister to others. Keep relying on God for your daily strength. Give Him thanks for His grace and promise of eternal life and peace. Jesus said, "Peace I leave with you; my peace I give you. I do not give to you as the world gives. Do not let your hearts be troubled and do not be afraid" (John 14:27, NIV).

"*Even though I walk through the [valley of the shadow of death], I will fear no evil, for you are with me; your rod and your staff, they comfort me*" (Psalm 23:4, NIV).

Notes

1. Hope for the Heart, "Terminal Illness," Quick Reference Counseling Keys Excerpt, http://www.hopefortheheart.org/pdfs/OLQR-pr-Terminal%20Illness.pdf.

2. Ibid.

3. Thomas J. Wooten, *Seasoned with Salt: Seasoned for the Day of Redemption* (North Charleston, SC: CreateSpace Independent Publishing, 2015), 176-180.

Chapter 3

The Response of the Church to the Spiritual Needs of the Terminally Ill

Man that is born of a woman is of few days and full of trouble.
(Job 14:1)

    The church has a responsibility to every member on its roll to watch over, to pray for, to exhort, and for the members to stir up each other unto every good work. How is that accomplished with the terminally ill and their families? What ongoing consistent spiritual care is provided for the person who is dying? What does the church provide for the person's family members? In the care of persons dealing with end-of-life issues I am often sought out to help patients, family members, and colleagues understand the spiritual and ethical values related to

- hope when there is no cure.
- personal autonomy and human dignity at the end of life.
- management of and assistance with spiritual concerns such as grief, prayer, feelings of hopelessness, pain, and death.

    Sorrow and grief are never easy. The church and well-wishers must remember that not all help is helpful. Jesus said "I am the way," not "I am in the way." Dying people have rights, needs, and concerns; their cries for help are often brushed aside and ignored because someone cannot deal with their own issues/fears/problems, or because they are not capable of meeting the person's needs. What are the spiritual needs of the sick and those who are terminally ill?

- **Community.** This includes church members, board members, co-workers, family, and friends.
- **To tell one's own story to an active listener.** That is someone who will sit and listen, someone who can be quiet and non-judgmental. It is someone who wants to be there with them.
- **Reconciliation.** There is a need to reconnect the past and connect the dots and close the gap. It may be one month or twenty years. The need to close the circle and reconnect is a given.
- **Meaning and purpose in life.** There is a strong need to experience hope even when surrounded by death.
- **Forgiveness.** Forgiveness for injuries to family members, co-workers, children, the church, and self.
- **Awareness of God.** Job 23:3 says, "Oh that I knew where I might find him!" In the midst of his darkness and distress Job looked for God.
- **To connect with God.** Both the patient and family need this and can accomplish it through prayers, genuine friendships, and Holy Communion. Brokenness, hurt, pain, and loss must be expressed, and only God can fill those needs. Only the grace of God can remove the lifelong stains of guilt and grief.
- **To feel that someone is in control.** They need to feel God's power. In this hour, the need for confession is paramount. Abandonment, alienation, and the fear of being punished are oftentimes supplanted with the need for liberation, to be freed from some form of bondage, and a stronger need for inspiration, positive motivation, and hopeful enthusiasm.

The Five Things that Terminally Ill Patients Need

The needs of the dying or terminally ill patient are as numerous and varied as the individuals. They want their families, their pastor, friends, and church to understand that they know what is going on with them, too. They know they are dying. Here are five (there are many more) basic things that every dying patient must have:

1. They must have help to make sense out of what is happening to them.
2. They need help to receive some sort of recognition that their life has meaning.
3. They want companionship; they do not want to be left alone. They do not want to die alone.
4. They want help. They need help in order to die appropriately. They want to die with dignity and respect and peace. Terminally ill patients' reactions to dying involve their struggles through the process of denial, anger, bargaining, depression, and acceptance. Ultimately, hope is the one attitude that they need in order to die appropriately.
5. They want to be given hope. They need to be given emotional and social support. They need to be touched and given a sense of control over their situation. They need someone to talk with about what they want to talk about. They want to feel a sense of self-importance in their last hours.

The Church's Response

When death is near, the pastor, the family, and the church must be willing, ready, and able to offer four critical steps in the process of dying. Mrs. Edwina Taylor, executive director of Cahaba Valley Health Care in Birmingham, Alabama, says, "When a person dies it takes a whole lot of pulling together."[1] She offers these four steps as healthy tasks for ministry in the final days and hours of life:

- **The Power of Presence** — Never abandon people. Remember, Jesus said "Lo, I am with you always" (Matthew 28:20).
- **Affirmation of Family** — Involve the person's family into the dying process. If the person was an active church member,

allow the family of faith to affirm the person as they transition to be with the Lord. Now is the time for family to be family. BE THERE.

- **Explain, Explain, Explain** — Communication is critical. Explain what is happening, and explain it again and again if necessary. Talking through the numbness, pain, agony, and shock can ease or help to eliminate emotional trauma.

- **Physical and Emotional Touch** — Death is not a time for boundaries. Touch, hold, and cry out the grief, agony, and pain.

The family of faith can also help the dying person by being especially sensitive to their needs. That is accomplished by gaining an inner understanding, respecting the person's wishes, rights, and desires, and your giving of yourself to them. By gaining an inner understanding, we look inwardly at our own feelings about death so we can better understand how the dying person feels. Respecting the rights of others involves the following:

- Go along with their anger, guilt, denial, and grief.
- Don't take things personally, or don't reinforce their denials. By sharing respect for the dying persons' rights, we can help them to relieve their guilt and help them rationalize their needs or desires to bargain by allowing them to see that some of their wishes can come true. Ultimately, a big part of this respect involves the persons' acceptance of death as a reality.
- By giving of ourselves, we as members of the household of faith can help meet physical needs that the dying person may have. Running errands, playing music, reading to them, praying with them, or simply just being there for them are simple yet impactful ways to demonstrate our sensitivity and understanding. We can also help by being open about death and by listening to them ramble on and on or by helping them to conduct some unfinished business that they may have.

- Their needs, wishes, and desires are the driving factors involved, not yours or anyone else's. Be there! Be open! Be prayerful!

Death and life are facts. Usually, a person's attitude toward death indicates what kind of life he or she lives or has lived. The Word of God teaches that death is a bridge between this life and the next. As the Herbert Wernecke poem states, "When God calls home a tired soul . . . This, too, is birth, not death."

Note

1. Wendy Murray Zoba, "Dying in Peace," *Christianity Today* (October 2001), http://www.christianitytoday.com/ct/2001/october22/9.80.html.

Chapter 4

Grief Resolution

And though after my skin worms destroy this body, yet in my flesh shall I see God. (Job 19:26)

Good folk and innocent people are not without their share of suffering—and often through no fault of their own. They are not immune to hard times. Indeed, believers can experience pain just as severely as nonbelievers. Being a child of God does not exempt one from anguish or from the heaviness of sorrow that bends the heart near the point of breaking.
(J. Grant Swank Jr.)

"You gave me life and showed me kindness, and in your providence watched over my spirit." (Job 10:12, NIV)

But when the kindness and love of God our Savior appeared, he saved us, not because of righteous things we had done, but because of his mercy. He saved us through the washing of rebirth and renewal by the Holy Spirit. (Titus 3:4-5, NIV)

Helping Others to Mourn

From the first chapters of Genesis to the last chapter in Revelation, grief and grief-related issues are prevalent and play an important part in the God-humanity story. Grief is one of those life factors that cuts across all races, creeds, colors, and sexes. All grieving people share a common bond. No one can get through life without loss and grief.

What should the chaplain/pastor/preacher say when someone's life has spun out of control, when a heart is broken and bleeding, when emotions are out of control, when the spirit is crushed, and when a person's life is in shambles? I dare say that it must be something that will restore those broken hearts and revive a life that has been turned upside-down. In times of grief, God does promise us something. Psalm 34:19 proclaims the compelling truth and promises of God: "Many are the afflictions of the righteous: but the LORD delivereth him out of them all." What is the role, duty, or responsibility of God's spokesperson? Luke 4:18-19 has the answer: "The Spirit of the Lord is upon me, because he hath anointed me to preach the gospel to the poor; he hath sent me to heal the brokenhearted, to preach deliverance to the captives, and recovering of sight to the blind, to set at liberty them that are bruised, to preach the acceptable year of the Lord."

First of all, the chaplain/pastor/preacher must be able to assist the person to somehow reconnect or reestablish himself/herself with God. Second, help the person find the courage and strength to tell their story by speaking the unspeakable. Third, help the person to write, talk, paint, cry, scream, dance, or yell out their problems. Help them develop communication skills to talk about/through the problem. Fourth, give them the tools to become empowered; help them to identify their feelings and separate their feelings from their thoughts. Fifth, help them to move from a place where they don't have to wear black or actively grieve. Isaiah 61:1-3 reads as follows:

> The Spirit of the Lord God is upon me; because the Lord hath anointed me to preach good tidings unto the meek; he hath sent me to bind up the brokenhearted, to proclaim liberty to the captives, and the opening of the prison to them that are bound; to proclaim the acceptable year of the Lord, and the day of vengeance

of our God; to comfort all that mourn; to appoint unto them that mourn in Zion, to give unto them beauty for ashes, the oil of joy for mourning, the garment of praise for the spirit of heaviness; that they might be called trees of righteousness, the planting of the Lord, that he might be glorified.

Grief has a way of immobilizing people. Hurt, pain, loss, death, and grief have a devastating way of destroying one's spiritual well-being. Grief-related issues will remain as they are and will not heal until the person can attach some meaning and spiritual emphasis and understanding to the matter. The wise and perceptive chaplain/pastor/preacher will see that void and find a way to provide a spiritual haven for the brokenhearted and grief-stricken soul. That is the aim of grief resolution. Spiritual healing must be the goal of grief recovery. Jesus said, "I am the way" (John 14:6a). Too many clergy members are in the way! They prevent healing, health, and hope from occurring. They are in the way of rest, restoration, and peace of mind, body, and soul. Their good intentions are too often in the way.

Grief is a natural process in response to a loss. Perhaps through deepening our human capacity to respond to each other in times of grief, we can continue to enrich each moment of our living. Grief is a process, and as a result is not a specific emotion like fear or sadness, but indeed is a constellation of a variety of thoughts, feelings, and behaviors. Grief is the internal meaning given to an external event. The capacity to provide grieving people with a sense of feeling understood is at the heart of all effective counseling.

DEFINITION OF TERMS
- **Bereavement:** Being deprived of a loved one's presence caused by loss such as death.

- **Grief:** Emotional suffering caused by death or another form of unusual loss.
- **Mourning:** The outward expression of grief and bereavement; it is "grief gone public" or "sharing one's grief outside of oneself."
- **Anticipatory Grief:** Grief that is expressed in advance of a loss when the loss is perceived as inevitable.
- **Acute Grief:** The intense grief which immediately follows the loss.
- **Grief Work:** The activity (or activities) associated with thinking through the loss, facing its reality, expressing the feelings and emotions experienced, and becoming reinvolved with life.

The Grief Stages

The stages of grief that people go through are normal and can be immediate or postponed. People in mourning should be encouraged to do their grief work.

- **STAGE 1: Shock**
  Shock is our temporary anesthesia, our temporary escape from reality. How do we help at this point? Be near the person and available to help, but do not take away from the person what they can do for themselves. The sooner they have to make some decisions and deal with the immediate problem, the better off they will be.

- **STAGE 2: Strong Emotion**
  We should not deny bereaved persons this outlet, for it is normal and helps in the healing process. Affirm or encourage the person to express emotions, whether it is through crying, talking it out, or some other commensurate emotional display.

- **STAGE 3: Depression and Loneliness**
  Be available to the person and let them know that whether they can believe it or not, this stage will pass too. In the midst of this loneliness, one may even feel isolated from God.

- **STAGE 4: Fear**
  Some symptoms of distress could be due to repressed emotions. Stressful times often dredge up other unresolved and repressed feelings, adding to the already overburdened emotional state.

- **STAGE 5: Panic**
  Uncertainty about ourselves and the future may set in because of the death being ever present in our minds.

- **STAGE 6: Guilt**
  This is almost a universal phenomenon. Often made are statements like "If only..."; "Why didn't I spend more time with...?"; and "Why didn't we call another doctor?" The person needs to be able to talk through these feelings with another person.

- **STAGE 7: Anger**
  A bereaved person might be angry at the doctor for not doing more; angry at the hospital staff for not being more attentive; and angry at the person who died. Then guilt and remorse sink in because of this spontaneous feeling. It helps people when they learn these reactions are normal. These feelings should be expressed.

- **STAGE 8: Apathy**
  It is hard for them to return to their regular routines. They begin a lot of activities but lose interest then switch to another project. Usual activities lose their importance. Further depression and loneliness accompany this stage. The usual activities were important only because they were done in connection with the deceased. The bereaving person may identify with the deceased and continue the projects or work of the deceased. In some cases, people begin having pains where the deceased experienced symptoms.

- **STAGE 9: Adjustment**
  Gradually, hope begins to return. There is still pain but the person begins to integrate the new reality of moving forward in life without the physical presence of the person who has died. A renewed sense of energy and confidence; an ability to fully acknowledge the reality of the death; and the capacity to become reinvolved with the normal activities of life slowly begin to appear.

- **STAGE 10: Struggle to Affirm Reality**
  This is the final stage, but it does not mean that the person becomes their old self again. A different person emerges on the other side of any grief experience. Depending on the response, they can come out a stronger or weaker individual.

Needs of a Grieving/Bereaved Person

A Safe Place. A brief change may be all right, but familiar surroundings are helpful.

Safe People. Friends, relatives, and a minister are necessary to give them the emotional support they need. It is better to have many short visits per week than one very long visit. Support without exhausting.

A Safe Situation. Any kind of safe situation that provides the bereaved person with worthwhile roles to perform will benefit. They should be uncomplicated and simple, and should not be likely to create anxiety. Asking for a cup of coffee can make them feel worthwhile and useful again.

Keys for Ministering at a Time of Grief

1. *Respect their emotional location.* Begin where the bereaved person is and not where you think they should be at this point in their life. Don't place your expectations for behavior on them.

2. *Clarify.* Get a clear understanding of feelings they have expressed.

3. *Empathize.* Feel with them.

4. *Be sensitive* to their feelings, and don't say too much.

5. *Listen with your heart.* Grieving is a matter of the heart rather than the head. Listening to the feelings of the person is the most important thing you can do. Don't try to find the right words because there are none. Your presence is more important than anything you can say.

6. *Accept all expressions of grief without censoring.* Often there are aggressive feelings expressed, including anger, resentment, guilt, and shame. Sometimes the person feels cheated by God. Let them be angry; God is big enough to handle it.

7. *Permit the person opportunity to talk openly about the departed loved one.* This is a vital part of the healing process. Enforced silence in this regard can be very detrimental and prevent acceptance.

8. *Remain available.* Be there; be available.

9. *Be sincere.* Think how you want to be treated, and always seek to be kind.

10. *Be realistic.* Don't use faulty reassurances with them.

11. *Don't desert.* After the initial impact of the loss, there is the tendency to leave the person alone.

12. *Don't try to fix the pain.* Suffering loss is painful. There must be pain before there can be healing (acceptance). The most difficult thing to learn about comforting is to permit the person to live their own pain. It is one thing to feel sorrow with a person but quite another thing to interfere with pain. Please allow the pain and at times the agony to occur in the person's life. Remember, there cannot be sunshine without rain.

Grief Avoidance Response Styles

Some respond to grief by attempting to avoid it altogether. In moving away from our feelings of grief, that is, in repressing, denying, or deadening our feelings, we ultimately become destructive to ourselves.

The destructive effects of the adopted pattern are typically directly proportional to the degree of avoidance. These avoidance responses are presented as various types or styles; they are not mutually exclusive. Some people will experience a combination of patterns, while others will maintain one primary mode of avoidance. Avoiding grief can be hazardous to your health and happiness.

A tremendous amount of anxiety, depression, and physical illness can be directly attributed to a person's quest to avoid their grief. Sleep difficulties, low self-esteem, chronic agitation, restlessness, and difficulty concentrating are other symptoms of grief avoidance. Below are five styles of grief avoidance.

1. **The Postponer** — A volcano ready to erupt. This person believes and is hopeful that if they delay the expression of their grief, over time it will go away. However, the grief builds up and usually comes out in unproductive ways. The goal of feeling safer is unrealized as the unresolved inner pain begs for expression.

2. **The Displacer** — A smoldering fire ready to ignite. This person shifts the expression of grief away from the loss itself and attaches it to a less-threatening person (usually self), place, or situation.

3. **The Replacer** — This person takes the emotions that were invested in the relationship that ended in death and reinvests the emotions prematurely in another relationship, work, or activity.

4. **The Minimizer** — A cripple walking on a broken leg. This person dilutes feelings of grief through a variety of rationalizations. Any feelings of grief are very threatening to the minimizer, who seeks to avoid pain at all costs. In an effort to quickly get over the grief, the minimizer represses feelings of grief; those feelings only continue to build within, and emotional strain results.

5. **The Somaticizer** — This person's feelings of grief convert into physical symptoms. They usually have a real need to be nurtured and comforted, whereas in taking on the "sick role" their emotional needs are met.[1]

The Grieving Process

The stages of mourning and grief are universal and are experienced by people from all walks of life. Mourning occurs in response to an individual's own terminal illness, the loss of a close relationship, or to the death of a valued being—human or animal. There are five stages of normal grief that were first proposed by Elisabeth Kübler-Ross in her 1969 book *On Death and Dying*. Kübler-Ross pioneered methods in the support and counselling of personal trauma, grief, and grieving associated with death and dying. She also dramatically improved the understanding and practices in relation to bereavement and hospice care. The five stages are listed below.

1. **Denial and Isolation**
   - Typical response: "This isn't true."
   - Denial functions as a buffer after unexpected shocking news.
   - People may isolate themselves from information or people that will confirm the death.
   - May become energetic in gathering proof from others that the death did not occur.

2. **Anger**
   - "Why me?"
   - Hostility, rage, envy, resentment, anger.
   - Difficult to deal with the person at this stage.
   - Anger should not be taken personally.

3. **Bargaining**
   - Want an extension on life, one more chance.
   - Period of self-delusion.
   - Normal attempt to postpone death.

- Person may need to deal with guilt or hidden emotions.
- Listen to person's concerns at this stage carefully.

4. **Depression**
   - Proof forces person to accept the loss; depression sets in and is normal.
   - Two kinds of depression are associated with grieving.
     - Reactive depression—reaction of the loss.
     - Preparatory depression—emotional preparation to give up everything.
   - Respond to the person with love, care, and empathy using few or no words.
   - Don't attempt to cheer up the person; doing so will interfere with the grief process.

5. **Acceptance**
   - Person feels tired, weak, finished with mourning.
   - Person begins to accept the death.
   - Stage is characterized by quiet peaceful resignation.
   - Person will draw inward; not a happy time.
   - Person doesn't need conversation in large crowds.
   - Show love, care, and support by being present; sit in silence or hold the person's hand.[2]

The Effect of Grief on the Human Body

Grief is a God-given, natural, healthy, self-corrective process. It is an ongoing, continuous, fluid process where people separate from someone or something that has been lost. A person that experiences grief may experience numbness, disbelief, denial, anger, rage, confusion, depression, guilt, and/or fear, and may vacillate between any of these. During the grief process these feelings can come in in waves, sometimes wave after wave of confusion, uncertainty, and fear. Disorientation and feelings of powerlessness run rampant. Light is often snuffed out by darkness. Joy is overcome with sadness.

Although everyone grieves differently, the responses vary according to temperament, background, emotional and physical health, age, the maturity of one's faith, and past losses. Of course there are additional factors that impact the person's response to loss. The current loss and time of grief can often trigger unresolved grief from past losses. Intense grief can and often does produce physical symptoms. Some people have complained about the following:

- Fatigue
- Shortness of breath
- Dizziness
- Palpitations
- Frequent ongoing feelings of numbness
- Irritability and restlessness
- Headaches and diarrhea
- Appetite loss
- Insomnia
- Inability to organize daily activities

Many grief-stricken individuals are often filled with self-blame; are preoccupied with the image of the deceased person, loss, guilt, feelings of not having done enough; and harbor hostility toward the medical staff, associates of the deceased, and those who attended to his or her care prior to death. Unresolved grief is often misidentified as

- a massive loss of energy.
- weight loss or gain.
- sense of unexplained emotional highs and lows.
- difficulty concentrating.

Pastor/Counselor Dos and Don'ts

During counseling sessions, I always remind myself that brokenhearted people drag a wagon filled with unresolved grief. As a result, I try to help them to let go and let God. Movement from hopelessness to hope, from midnight to midday, involves a long and painful journey. The pastor/counselor should observe that there are things that one should and should not do while accompanying persons on that journey. What are some of those dos and don'ts?

DO

- Remember, nothing you can say can stop a grieving person's pain.
- Remember to extend words of comfort, condolences, and prayers to the mourner's often-forgotten grandparents, siblings, stepchildren, aunts, uncles, cousins, friends, and anyone who is closely associated with the deceased.
- Remember that the most difficult time for the family is the seven to nine months after death.
- Remember them on holidays; the "firsts" can be especially painful.
- Remember that grief is long-lasting.
- Remember to always give the mourner permission to grieve.
- Remember to pray for them.
- Remember the grieving with a call, card, or letter (letters can be read and reread). Letters and cards are handwritten hugs that show you care.
- Remember to be a friend. It is their day today, but it could be yours tomorrow.
- Remember to allow the grieving person to talk about the deceased loved one.
- Remember, a sympathizing ear, a warm embrace, an arm around the shoulder, or a squeeze of the hand can demonstrate your concern and shows that you care.

DON'T
- Don't avoid the grieving person because you don't know what to say or do.
- Never say "don't cry" or "be brave." Allow the grieving person to grieve. They need to let it out.
- Don't encourage them to repress their feelings.
- Don't use clichés, or make trite statements or curt remarks. Never say things such as "time heals all wounds," or "the Lord knows best," "be glad it's over," or "she/he is at rest."
- Don't ever say "I know how you feel." People's relationships with their deceased are unique. You don't know how someone else is hurting. Never say it!
- Don't make statements or ask questions that induce guilt or cause blame. There will always be unfinished business and guilt associated with death.
- Don't change the subject or cut off discussions when the grieving person talks about his or her loved one.
- Don't tell the grieving person that his or her loss is God's gain, and never make any of the following related statements:
  - *He will get you in the end.*
  - *God numbered his/her days, and they ran out and God took him/her.*
  - *God must have needed another rose for His rose garden.*
  - *God knows best. He won't put any more on you than you can bear.*
- Don't try to answer the question "Why?"
- Don't encourage the grieving person to "get over it" because of your own discomfort with the person's depressed condition.
- Don't attempt to minimize the loss of a baby or child or young death. The age of the deceased makes no difference with the level of pain. The pain and grief are just as great.

"Surely he hath borne our griefs, and carried our sorrows: yet we did esteem him stricken, smitten of God, and afflicted. But he was wounded for our transgressions, he was bruised for our iniquities: the chastisement of our peace was upon him; and with his stripes we are healed" (Isaiah 53:4-5).

Notes to Pastors or Counselors: Helpee/Helper Sample Conversations

Note # 1 — Avoiding Attempts at Quick Solutions

When Martha heard that Jesus was coming, she went and met Him while Mary sat in the house. Martha said to Jesus, "Lord, if you had been here my brother would not have died, and even now I know that whatever you ask from God, God will give you." Jesus said to her, "Your brother will rise again. . . . I am the resurrection and the life; he who believes in me, though he die, yet shall he live, and whoever lives and believes in me shall never die."

Then Mary, when she came where Jesus was and saw Him, fell at His feet, saying to Him, "Lord, if you had been here, my brother would not have died." When Jesus saw her weeping, and the Jews who came with her also weeping, He was deeply moved in spirit and troubled; and He said, "Where have you laid him?" They said to Him, "Lord, come and see." Jesus wept, so the Jews said, "See how he loved him" (adapted from John 11).

Note #2 — What 1 Thessalonians 4:13 Says about Grieving

"Grieve not as those who have no hope."

Note #3 — What 1 Thessalonians 4:13 DOES NOT Say about Grieving

"Grieve not."

Note #4 — Simple but Profound Words
"I'm with you," or "I care and I'm here."

Note #5 — Don't Challenge the Denial
Helpee: "I can't believe he/she is dead."
Don't Say: "You will get used to it. It just takes time."
Do Say: "It's really hard to believe he/she is dead."

Helpee: "He/she can't be dead. He/she just can't. I know that I'm going to turn around and find him/her here again."
Don't Say: "You have to accept the fact that he/she is dead."
Do Say: "You sometimes expect to see him/her here."

Note #6 — An Example of How to Reflect Feelings of Grief
Helpee: "I can't bear the thought of living alone."
Helper: "You are feeling lonely already."
Helpee: "Yes. How can I live without him/her?"
Helper: "It seems to you like living without her/him will be hard now that he/she is gone."

Note #7 — When You Are at a Loss for Words
"I really don't know what to say. All I can say is, I'm with you."

Note #8 — Allow Helpees to Make Decisions
Helpee: "I'm so upset; I don't know what to do."
Helper: "It sounds like you have some decisions you need to make."
Helpee: "Yes, there is so much happening. For instance, I don't know if I should hire someone to help with the housework or try to do it myself. What do you think?"
Helper: "I'm really not positive what would be best for you. Do you have a preference?"

Helpee: "Yes, I really could use some help with the housework. There are some things I can't do."
Helper: "It sounds like you have made a decision."
Helpee: "Yes, I'll hire some help."

Note #9 — Assist Helpees to Avoid Making Rash Decisions
Helpee: "I've got to get out of this house. I've decided to move."
Helper: "That seems like a big decision."
Helpee: "There are just so many reminders of my wife/husband here. I just need to get away from all the painful memories."
Helper: "You experience a lot of pain remaining here and you think moving will be helpful."
Helpee: "Yes, I've got to get away."
(After further conversation)
Helper: "I can appreciate your desire to get away from those painful memories, but I would like to encourage you to delay your decision for a while. Moving can be a crisis in itself, and it might actually create more problems rather than solve old ones. Is it possible to decide on such a major decision when things have settled down some?"

Note #10 — The Therapeutic Value of Crying
Helper: "How have things been lately?"
Helpee: (Says nothing but looks as if he/she is holding back tears.)
Helper: "You haven't said much about all that has happened. I want to let you know that it is really all right to cry if you want to."

Note #11 — Facilitating Expression of Feelings
Helpee: "I really miss him/her so much. What will I do without him or her?"

Don't Say: "You'll get along somehow."

Do Say: "You must be feeling a deep sense of loss. He/she isn't here anymore, and you're really missing him/her. It's hard on you right now."

Note #12 — Accepting Feelings of Anger and Hostility

Helpee: "God must be absolutely horrible to have done this to me. I hate Him."

Don't Say: "Why, that's terrible of you to say that! Why are you so hostile?"

Do Say: "It sounds as if you're feeling pretty angry at God because of what happened. Could you tell me more about how you feel?"

Note #13 — Facilitating Expression of Guilt

Helpee: "I feel so terrible that he/she died before I could arrive at the hospital."

Don't Say: "Well, it's silly for you to feel bad about it. You couldn't make it. And that's just the way it is."

Do Say: "I can sense that you're having some guilt feelings about being absent when he/she died. Did you have something you wanted to say to him/her before he/she died?"

Note #14 — Acknowledge Realistic Guilt

"You've confessed to me your guilt in this matter. And I agree that it's pretty terrible. You're feeling really bad right now."

Note #15 — Platitudes to Avoid Saying

"God willed it."

"God only takes the good."

"Every cloud has a silver lining."

"Everything will be all right."

Note #16 — Gently Confront Platitudes of the Helpee

Helpee: "God must have willed it."

Helper: "Could you tell me more about that?"

Helpee: (After a thoughtful pause) "I guess I really don't know what I mean by that."

Helper: "It is really difficult to make sense out of all of this, isn't it?"

Helpee: "Yes, it is."

Note #17 — Speak to Platitudes of Others

Helper: "I noticed your friend told you not to worry because everything would turn out all right. It looked as if that bothered you."

Helpee: "Yes, it did. That's so easy for him/her to say, but he/she didn't lose his/her husband/wife."

Helper: "You don't think he/she really understands."

Helpee: "That's right. If he/she knew how I felt, he/she wouldn't have said that."

Helper: "It sounds as if that hurt you."

Helpee: "It did kind of hurt, even though I know he/she was trying to be helpful."

Note #18 — Concerned Follow-up Questions

"It's been over a year now since your husband/wife died. How are you managing?"

"How do you feel now when you think about your wife/husband?"

"Do you find yourself still missing your child as much as you used to?"

Stages of Grief Expanded

We referenced the five stages of normal grief that were first proposed by Elisabeth Kübler-Ross. The following chart further depicts the stages of the grief process as modeled by several influential psychologists. These are in columns for the purposes of comparison and thought. The grief process is not neat, predictable, or orderly. Most people experience most of these stages but may not do so in a set order. For most people, the minimum period to make a healthy adjustment to a major loss in their lives is about a year.

Response to Loss (Bowlby)	Stages of Dying (Kübler-Ross)	Grief Process (Westberg)	Response to Loss (Engel)	Synthesis
Protest (shock, disbelief, depression)	Denial / Isolation	Shock Emotional Display	Shock / Disbelief (denial, anxiety)	Shock / Disbelief
	Anger	Depression Physical Symptoms	Development of Awareness (anger, depression, guilt, blame)	Immobilization Despair
Despair	Bargaining	Panic Guilt		Acceptance Re-involvement
	Depression	Resentment Hope	Restitution (sadness, fears, changes)	
Detachment (letting go, reorganization of life)	Acceptance	Adjustment	Resolution (consequences, self-esteem, identity, issues/changes)	

Notes

1. Adapted from "Understanding Common Patterns of Avoiding Grief," by Alan D. Wolfelt, http://www.idhca.org/wp-content/uploads/2017/07/Hiles_Understanding-Common-Patterns-of-Grief-Avoidance.pdf.

2. Elizabeth Kübler-Ross, *On Death and Dying*, 1st ed. (New York: Macmillan Company, 1969), 38-137.

CHAPTER 5

Presenting Problems

The examples offered in this chapter are taken from myriad encounters with pastors that I have had over the past forty years. The hope is that they will provide something of value for you and your ministry or life. I have tried to demonstrate how devastating unresolved issues can be in the grieving process. The repercussions and repulsion can be quite extensive in terms of time, resources, and emotional strain if unresolved issues are not addressed and resolved head-on. The consequences can very often be beyond your imagination and belief. Much care must be taken to assess and then address those underlying issues during times of crisis. It is during a crisis that a pastor's spiritual and clinical training, skills, and insight are of utmost importance. It could ultimately mean the difference between life and death. My prayer for you, your ministry, and your people in the house of God, in the hospital, or in the home is one for success as you bring hope, healing, and help to the people of God. I have used an old tool for presenting these examples that has proved extremely helpful for the past thirty years:

First is the **Presenting Problem**. This is what is listed as the chief complaint and is the primary reason the person has requested help or hospitalization. The presenting problem may not be the most serious or even the one that will lead to the most serious outcome. It is a start and beginning in the process and encounter.

Second is the **Facts Bearing on the Problem**. These include the causes of the problem, the current problem, and the history of the problem, as well as how the problem impacts the person's life and/or family.

Third, I create **Long- and Short-term Goals and Objectives** for growth, development, improvement, and sustainability.

Fourth, I establish **Therapeutic Interventions** in an attempt to provide a remedy to assist in relief of the presenting problem. These are suggested actions to consider from a spiritual and/or clinical perspective. They are offered as possible or potential reasons for a referral if needed. The medical issues are not addressed here; they will be taken up by the medical team.

Fifth and last, I prepare **Notes** to the pastors and counselors regarding potential areas of concern.

Presenting Problem in the Hospital: End-of-life/Terminal Illness[1]
Facts Bearing on the Problem
1. A family member or close friend is diagnosed with a life-threatening or terminal illness.
2. The medical program indicates a slow and progressive deterioration.
3. Family conflicts develop because of the illness.
4. Feelings of helplessness and hopelessness surface as tension grows.

Pastoral or Counselor Goals and Objectives
1. Due to the uncertainty of time and progressiveness of the illness, assist the family in verbalizing their feelings about the illness, the loved one, and treatment plan.
2. Allow family members to share their thoughts, feelings, and impact the crisis has on them.

3. Allow the family member who is ill an opportunity to see the family members working together and praying for unity and peace among themselves.
4. Work out a family visitation schedule and inform the family member who is ill.
5. Provide spiritual and emotional help as needed.

Pastoral or Counselor Therapeutic Intervention
1. **Consider Hospice or Palliative Care.** Most people are not aware of the difference between hospice and palliative care.
   - **Hospice care** is for patients with life-threatening illnesses who can no longer benefit from regular treatment and who generally have six months or less to live as determined by a doctor. Hospice care provides reasonable and necessary medical and support services to patients with terminal illnesses. Hospice treatment focuses on treating the symptoms of a disease rather than the disease itself. Attention and care are focused on helping the patient maintain the highest possible quality of life. Hospice care is given in three types of facilities: (1) an institutional facility for hospice care; (2) care at home; or (3) an assisted-living facility, hospital, or nursing home.
   - **Palliative care** is designed for patients who want and need comfort at any stage of any illness. It does not matter whether the illness is terminal or chronic.
2. **Suggest taking a spiritual inventory as death approaches.** Dr. Kathleen Dowling Singh said, "The fact of death is the great mystery and the great truth that illuminates our lives. To face our eminent death is to examine our lives with an urgency and honesty we may never have felt before."[2]

As we take stock of our own lives and realistically and honestly learn where we are, here are some questions to consider.

- Who have I been all this time?
- How have I used my gift of human life?
- What do I need to "clear up" or "let go of" in order to be more peaceful?
- What gave my life meaning?
- For what am I grateful?
- What have I learned of truth, and how truthful have I learned to be?
- What have I learned of love and how have I learned to show love?
- What have I learned about tenderness, vulnerability, intimacy, and communion?
- What have I learned about courage, strength, power, and faith?
- What have I learned of the human condition, and how great is my compassion?
- How am I handling my suffering?
- With whom can I best share what I've learned?
- What helps me open my heart and empty my mind and experience the presence of God's Spirit?
- What will give me strength as I die? What is my relationship with that which gives me strength as I die?
- If I remembered that my breaths were numbered, what would be my relationship to this breath right now?
- Who am I?[3]

Notes for Pastors and Counselors

It would be most helpful to the patient and selected family members if they would engage in some family activities such as writing a journal or organizing a family photo album. And finally, it is critical and most necessary that family, close friends, and spiritual leaders are with the dying person. Saying goodbye is a demonstration of love that will last forever.

Presenting Problem in the Hospital or Home: Suicide Ideation[4]
Facts Bearing on the Problem
1. The patient has current thoughts of or preoccupation with death or hurting himself/herself.
2. The patient does not have a plan in place, yet continues to think about death.
3. The patient has recently attempted suicide.
4. The patient has a history of suicide attempt(s) that required hospitalization and medication.
5. The patient's family has a history of suicide or suicide attempts.
6. The patient admits to being depressed and dejected with life and his/her surroundings.

Pastoral or Counselor Long-term Goals and Objectives
1. First, stabilize the patient and assess his/her crisis.
2. Ensure that the patient has sufficient and proper care.
3. Work to instill hope and positive thoughts in/with the patient.

Pastoral or Counselor Short-term Goals and Objectives
1. Help the patient identify and discuss the problems and causes of these life stressors.
2. Work to assist the patient in verbalizing suicidal feelings and thoughts as much as possible.
3. Work to assist patient in discussing positive reasons for living.
4. Ensure the patient's ongoing safety (physically, emotionally, and spiritually).

Pastoral or Counselor Therapeutic Interventions and Plan of Action
1. Make an assessment plan to track the reasons for this present crisis.

2. Assist the patient's family and provide spiritual and pastoral care as needed.
3. Encourage the patient to join a support group.
4. Encourage the patient to make a "safety first" contract when he/she develops feelings or thoughts that lead to suicidal thoughts.
5. Encourage patient to take medications as prescribed.
6. During counseling sessions with the patient explore reasons, thoughts, and feelings that led to his/her crisis.

Notes for Pastor or Counselor
This person may possibly have a borderline personality disorder and may need a referral.

Presenting Problem in the Hospital or Home: Combination of Medical Issues[5]

Facts Bearing on the Problem
1. The patient has several serious medical problems that he/she has neglected.
2. The patient has a concurring issue with alcohol and mental health problems.

Pastoral or Counselor Long-term Goals and Objectives
1. Encourage the patient to follow doctor's orders until his/her condition has been stabilized.
2. Assist the patient to address any ongoing crisis that impacts his/her life.
3. Encourage the patient to begin treatment to address the recurring problems.

Pastoral or Counselor Short-term Goals and Objectives
1. Provide patient with assistance in the compliance with all medical tests, medication, and follow-up requirements and plans.
2. Assist the patient with the knowledge, understanding of, and impact of alcohol and drugs on his/her medical condition.
3. Assist the patient on the impact of unresolved mental health problems and their effect on his/her life.
4. Assist the patient in the development of coping skills and how to identify the onset of medical problems and to take corrective action.

Pastoral or Counselor Therapeutic Interventions and Plan of Action
1. Assist the patient with an established plan of action for clarification, identification, and follow-through with all prescribed plans.
2. Encourage the patient to seek support from all support groups and be transparent and open to new possibilities for help, healing, and health.
3. Assist patient by working with medical team (following an established treatment plan to ensure a healthy and prosperous life of sobriety and mental clarity).

Notes for Pastors or Counselors
This patient may be a candidate for a referral for pain disorder associated with psychological factors. Also, the concurring disorders must be addressed. Are there any family issues that require your immediate attention?

Presenting Problem in the Hospital and Home: Death of Family Member or Spouse[6]

Facts Bearing on the Problem
1. The patient was informed that a family member or spouse has died.
2. Feelings of guilt, shame, and anger over the loss.
3. Anger, out-of-control emotions and feelings toward God for allowing this death to occur.

Pastoral or Counselor Long-term Goals and Objectives
1. Assist the family member to begin the grieving process.
2. Allow the family member to talk about his/her feelings, emotions, and frustrations.
3. Help the family member to resolve his/her anger at God and perhaps other family members as the grieving continues.

Pastoral or Counselor Short-term Goals and Objectives
1. Assist the family member to accept the loss of his/her loved one or spouse.
2. Begin to make the necessary arrangements.
3. Help him/her to put his/her feelings and emotions into words.
4. Meet with other family members and address all pertinent and immediate concerns and grief-related issues.
5. Encourage the family member(s) to join a support group for help, hope, and encouragement.
6. Guide the family member through the steps of grief with an understanding that the steps are not placed in stone; feelings and emotions are fluid and can go up or down at any time.

Pastoral or Counselor Therapeutic Interventions and Plan of Action

1. Offer immediate help and/or support as needed.
2. Notify other support persons or groups to provide additional support and assistance.
3. Offer any support and guidance you deem necessary to assist the family or spouse.
4. Offer prayer and words of comfort.

Notes for Pastors or Counselors

1. Remember to be with the spouse or family at times like these/this.
2. Remember to keep a prayerful and positive outlook and attitude at all times.
3. Remember the actions of Jesus at Lazarus's grave in John 11:35—"Jesus wept." Jesus loved His friend and demonstrated that love and concern. Remember that fact. Today may be your time to help; tomorrow is another day.

Presenting Problem in the Home: Balancing the Demands of Work, Family, and Personal Issues[7]

Facts Bearing on the Problem

1. The family has been overwhelmed with internal fighting over the demands of work, home, and personal issues.
2. Infighting has caused resentments, hurt feelings, and division.
3. Lack of communication and deception have caused the family system to be totally divided in a combative, divisive, and unhappy, unhealthy environment.

Pastoral or Counselor Long-term Goals and Objectives

1. Help to move the family unit to a safe and healthy place.
2. Help them to establish a plan of action where they can agree to disagree.

Pastoral or Counselor Short-term Goals and Objectives
1. Meet with each family member individually to assess their issues and concerns.
2. Seek a solution where the entire family agrees to participate.
3. Have each family member to share their own feelings, hurts, and how the problems impact them.
4. Seek an agreement where each family member agrees to change something in their behavior that is an irritant to other family members.
5. Work to find a place of safety for each member of the family when discussing work, family matters, and personal needs.

Pastoral or Counselor Therapeutic Interventions and Plan of Action
1. Meet with the family unit as a whole to lay out the issues that need resolution.
2. Encourage each family member to seek God's face as they move toward resolution and eventually closure.
3. Seek clarification of each member's needs, specific behavioral changes each person will make, and how they will forgive other family members for hurts and pain caused.

Notes for Pastor or Counselor
Remember to allow each family equal time and opportunity to share their issues, clarify their needs, and ensure that other family members understand their needs.

Presenting Problem in the Home: How to Restore a Broken Relationship after an Affair[8]
Facts Bearing on the Problem
1. One of the marriage partners had an affair.
2. The marriage is in serious trouble.

3. Some of the types of problems could include infidelity, jealousy, physical, psychological, and mental abuse, and/or sexual abuse.

Pastoral or Counselor Long-term Goals and Objectives
1. Reestablish an open line of communication between the marriage partners.
2. Restore trust and rebuild accountability and faith between the partners.

Pastoral or Counselor Short-term Goals and Objectives
1. Find a way to help the one who was injured by the affair a way to grieve the loss of fidelity and trust and move to a place of hope.
2. Allow the one who was hurt an opportunity to vent and discuss their feelings about and disappointments in the actions of his/her partner.

Pastoral or Counselor Therapeutic Interventions and Plan of Action
1. Establish boundaries that are clear and safe for both partners.
2. If the marriage can be saved, admit that and agree to work toward a reconciliation that is agreeable to both of them.
3. Rebuild accountability.
4. Allow the violator to confess, admit his/her actions, and explain why they violated the marriage vow.
5. Allow the violator to seek forgiveness from his/her partner.

Notes for the Pastor or Counselor
This situation represents a very serious grievance and violation of the marriage vows. It must be handled in an extremely sensitive and serious manner and requires much prayer.

Presenting Problem in the Home: Uncertainty about What Couples Need from Each Other in a Marriage[9]

Facts Bearing on the Problem

1. The couple consistently questions why they got married.
2. Their arguments always end up with a discussion about their children and their bond/union.
3. These types of problems arise out of a sense of disillusionment with the marriage, infidelity, some major life-changing event or events, jealousy, loss of love and affection, midlife crisis, personality differences, or desire to move on with a separation and eventual divorce.

Pastoral or Counselor Long- and Short-term Goals and Objectives

1. Assist the couple in remembering how they met and initially began dating.
2. Have them to seek out ways and means to recount and reclaim the goals and ideals they had for their future.
3. Help them to clarify what they need, what they want, and how their partner can help them to obtain those things.

Pastoral or Counselor Therapeutic Interventions Are Based upon These Questions for the Couple

1. How will you know therapy has been successful and has rekindled a desire for your mate?
2. What has been the cause or reason for the change(s) in your relationship? And what are you willing to do to restore it?
3. What will you do to encourage change in your mate?

Presenting Problem in the Home and Church: Suffering from Survivor's Guilt[10]

Facts Bearing on the Problem
1. Many young veterans return home from war and suffer from survivor's guilt.
2. They struggle with guilty feelings for surviving or being injured when some of their friends or comrades were killed or seriously injured.
3. They seek spiritual healing and help, yet they are angry with God.
4. They may feel they are worthless and good for nothing and need to die.

Pastoral or Counselor Long-term Goals or Objectives
1. Remove the guilty feelings and thoughts of dying.
2. Help the person to regain self-esteem and positive thoughts and feelings about himself or herself.
3. Assist the person to understand that death is part and parcel of life.

Pastoral or Counselor Short-term Goals and Objectives
1. Help the person to identify and name his/her reasons for the guilty feelings.
2. Help him/her to become as open and honest and transparent about the concerns as possible.
3. Allow him/her to have a complete catharsis.
4. As the person works with his/her therapist, assist him/her in finding a safe place to admit and accept that grief, death, loss, guilt, and feelings of self-blame are all normal feelings in life.

Pastoral or Counselor Therapeutic Interventions and Plan of Action

1. Move toward a therapeutic relationship where the person feels safe with you and is willing to share his/her troubling feelings and thoughts.
2. Move the person in a positive and careful way to discuss the troubling incident in as much detail as possible.
3. Encourage the person to share as much history about his/her problems and allow him/her to go as deeply as possible into their feelings and emotions.

Notes for Pastors and Counselors

This situation could have multiple ongoing themes that are entangled and twisted into the person's psyche. Bereavement, death and dying, adjustment disorder, alcohol dependency/abuse, major depression, and post-traumatic stress disorder are a few.

Presenting Problem in the Home or Hospital: Post-traumatic Stress Disorder (PTSD)[11]

Facts Bearing on the Problem

1. The person has been exposed to a traumatic event involving actual or perceived threat of death or serious injury.
2. He/she reports disturbing and persistent thoughts, images, and/or perceptions of the traumatic event.
3. Describes a reliving of the event, particularly through flashbacks.
4. The person has feelings of intense fear, helplessness, or horror of the traumatic event.

Pastoral or Counselor Long-term Goal and Objectives
1. Help the person to remove or eliminate the thoughts and feelings from his/her life.
2. Move the person toward a return to their original level of thinking and feeling prior to the traumatic event.

Pastoral or Counselor Short-term Goals and Objectives
1. Help the person to move toward healing by talking through his/her fears and thoughts.
2. Have the person to describe his/her feelings and thoughts and their impact on his/her life.
3. Help the person to replace the negative thoughts with positive and encouraging thoughts.

Notes to the Pastor or Counselor
Working with a PTSD patient can be difficult, demanding, and challenging. Stay the course and have a well laid-out plan. Be very prayerful. A final word and suggestion for pastors and spiritual caregivers who work with emotionally distressed and suspected mentally ill members: Remember the difference between flight, freeze, and fight responses. The freeze response is the most common of the three. In this response, the person does not do anything to deal with the situation. The person will put distance between themselves and the situation because of their feelings of being powerless and their inability to meet the emotional, relational, and physical intimacy requirements/needs of the other person or situation. The flight response is one of avoidance. Some examples might include taking sick leave from work or keeping a low, out-of-the-way profile or staying away from the person or situation. The final response is the fight response. It involves being assertive and fighting back. Consider these critical skills necessary for pastors and spiritual caregivers:

- Pastors and spiritual caregivers must be vigilant, attentive, and careful in dealing with these types of situations. I have discovered that people are like icebergs, which show only 10 percent of its structure above the surface.
- Clergy and spiritual caregivers should have a working knowledge of the different types of mental disorders and know when to make a referral.
- Clergy and spiritual caregivers need to know the times when a church member or person who is involved in a mental health crisis only needs some support and encouragement. There are times when church members, family members, friends, and others who are faced with anxiety symptoms simply need help to face their phobias, fears, and issues at that time in their lives.
- Clergy members and spiritual leaders should become familiar with the techniques, skills, and tools that will enable them to recognize the symptoms associated with the crisis or mental illness.

Notes

1. Arthur E. Jongsma and Frank M. Dattilio, *The Family Therapy Treatment Planner* (New York: John Wiley & Sons, 2000), 230-236.

2. Kathleen Dowling Singh, PhD, "Taking a Spiritual Inventory," National Caregivers Library, http://www.caregiverslibrary.org/caregivers-resources/grp-end-of-life-issues/taking-a-spiritual-inventory-article.aspx.

3. Ibid.

4. Robert R. Perkinson and Arthur E. Jongsma Jr., *The Chemical Dependence Treatment Planner* (New York: John Wiley & Sons, 1998), 226-233.

5. James R. Kok and Arthur E. Jongsma Jr., *The Pastoral Counseling Treatment Planner* (New York: John Wiley & Sons, 1998), 96-154.

6. Ibid.

7. Jongsma and Dattilio, *Family Therapy*, 156-162.

8. Gary Schultheis, Steffanie O'Hanlon, and Bill O'Hanlon, *Couples Therapy Homework Planner,* 2nd ed., series editor Arthur E. Jongsma Jr. (New York: John Wiley & Sons, 2010), 118-119.

9. Ibid., 162-164.

10. Bret A. Moore and Arthur E. Jongsma Jr., *The Veterans and Active Duty Military Psychotherapy Treatment Planner* (New York: John Wiley & Sons, 2009), 274-279.

11. Ibid., 206-215.

CHAPTER 6

Bible Verses Quick Reference

Comfort for the Terminally Ill

2 Kings 20:1, NIV—*In those days Hezekiah became ill and was at the point of death. The prophet Isaiah son of Amoz went to him and said, "This is what the LORD says: 'Put your house in order, because you are going to die; you will not recover.'"*

Psalm 23:4, NIV—*Even though I walk through the [valley of the shadow of death], I will fear no evil, for you are with me; your rod and your staff, they comfort me.*

Psalm 139:16, NIV—*Your eyes saw my unformed body; all the days ordained for me were written in your book before one of them came to be.*

Matthew 6:27, NIV—*"Can any one of you by worrying add a single hour to your life?"*

John 5:24, NIV—*"Very truly I tell you, whoever hears my word and believes him who sent me has eternal life and will not be judged but has crossed over from death to life."*

Romans 8:6, NIV—*The mind governed by the flesh is death, but the mind governed by the Spirit is life and peace.*

Philippians 1:21, NIV—*For to me, to live is Christ and to die is gain.*

John 14:1-4—*Let not your heart be troubled: ye believe in God, believe also in me. In my Father's house are many mansions: if it were not so, I would have told you. I go to prepare a place for you. And if I go and prepare a place for you, I will come again, and receive you unto myself; that where I am, there ye may be also. And whither I go ye know, and the way ye know.*

Romans 8:16-17—*The Spirit itself beareth witness with our spirit, that we are the children of God: and if children, then heirs; heirs of God, and joint-heirs with Christ; if so be that we suffer with him, that we may be also glorified together.*

2 Corinthians 5:6-8—*Therefore we are always confident, knowing that, whilst we are at home in the body, we are absent from the Lord: (For we walk by faith, not by sight:) We are confident, I say, and willing rather to be absent from the body, and to be present with the Lord.*

1 Thessalonians 4:16-18—*For the Lord himself shall descend from heaven with a shout, with the voice of the archangel, and with the trump of God: and the dead in Christ shall rise first: Then we which are alive and remain shall be caught up together with them in the clouds, to meet the Lord in the air: and so shall we ever be with the Lord. Wherefore comfort one another with these words.*

1 Thessalonians 5:9-11—*For God hath not appointed us to wrath, but to obtain salvation by our Lord Jesus Christ, who died for us, that, whether we wake or sleep, we should live together with him. Wherefore comfort yourselves together, and edify one another, even as also ye do.*

2 Samuel 12:23—*But now he is dead, wherefore should I fast? can I bring him back again? I shall go to him, but he shall not return to me.* (King David speaking of his young son who died)

John 11:23-26, NIV—*Jesus said to her, "Your brother will rise again." Martha answered, "I know he will rise again in the resurrection at the last day." Jesus said to her, "I am the resurrection and the life. The one who believes in me will live, even though they die; and whoever lives by believing in me will never die. Do you believe this?"*

1 Corinthians 15:54-57, NIV—*When the perishable has been clothed with the imperishable, and the mortal with immortality, then the saying that is written will come true: "Death has been swallowed up in victory." "Where, O death, is your victory? Where, O death, is your sting?" The sting of death is sin, and the power of sin is the law. But thanks be to God! He gives us the victory through our Lord Jesus Christ.*

Philippians 3:20-21, NIV—*But our citizenship is in heaven. And we eagerly await a Savior from there, the Lord Jesus Christ, who, by the power that enables him to bring everything under his control, will transform our lowly bodies so that they will be like his glorious body.*

1 Corinthians 15:20-23—*But now is Christ risen from the dead, and become the firstfruits of them that slept. For since by man came death, by man came also the resurrection of the dead. For as in Adam all die, even so in Christ shall all be made alive. But every man in his own order: Christ the firstfruits; afterward they that are Christ's at his coming.*

Philippians 1:23-24, NIV—*I am torn between the two: I desire to depart and be with Christ, which is better by far; but it is more necessary for you that I remain in the body.*

1 Peter 1:3-5—*Blessed be the God and Father of our Lord Jesus Christ, which according to his abundant mercy hath begotten us again unto a lively hope by the resurrection of Jesus Christ from the dead, to an inheritance incorruptible, and undefiled, and that fadeth not away, reserved in heaven for you, who are kept by the power of God through faith unto salvation ready to be revealed in the last time.*

1 John 3:1-2—*Behold, what manner of love the Father hath bestowed upon us, that we should be called the sons of God: therefore the world knoweth us not, because it knew him not. Beloved, now are we the sons of God, and it doth not yet appear what we shall be: but we know that, when he shall appear, we shall be like him; for we shall see him as he is.*

Revelation 21:1-4—*And I saw a new heaven and a new earth: for the first heaven and the first earth were passed away; and there was no more sea. And I John saw the holy city, new Jerusalem, coming down from God out of heaven, prepared as a bride adorned for her husband. And I heard a great voice out of heaven saying, Behold, the tabernacle of God is with men, and he will dwell with them, and they shall be his people, and God himself shall be with them, and be their God. And God shall wipe away all tears from their eyes; and there shall be no more death, neither sorrow, nor crying, neither shall there be any more pain: for the former things are passed away.*

Psalm 116:15—*Precious in the sight of the* L{\scriptsize ORD} *is the death of his saints.*

John 10:27-29, NIV—*"My sheep listen to my voice; I know them, and they follow me. I give them eternal life, and they shall never perish; no one will snatch them out of my hand. My Father, who has given them to me, is greater than all; no one can snatch them out of my Father's hand."*

Romans 8:38-39—*For I am persuaded, that neither death, nor life, nor angels, nor principalities, nor powers, nor things present, nor things to come, nor height, nor depth, nor any other creature, shall be able to separate us from the love of God, which is in Christ Jesus our Lord.*

Romans 14:8—*For whether we live, we live unto the Lord; and whether we die, we die unto the Lord: whether we live therefore, or die, we are the Lord's.*

Revelation 14:13, NIV—*Then I heard a voice from heaven say, "Write this: Blessed are the dead who die in the Lord from now on." "Yes," says the Spirit, "they will rest from their labor, for their deeds will follow them."*

Words of Comfort and Hope for Sick and Shut-ins

Psalm 103:13-22—*Like as a father pitieth his children, so the LORD pitieth them that fear him. For he knoweth our frame; he remembereth that we are dust. As for man, his days are as grass: as a flower of the field, so he flourisheth. For the wind passeth over it, and it is gone; and the place thereof shall know it no more. But the mercy of the LORD is from everlasting to everlasting upon them that fear him, and his righteousness unto children's children; to such as keep his covenant, and to those that remember his commandments to do them. The LORD hath prepared his throne in the heavens; and his kingdom ruleth over all. Bless the LORD, ye his angels, that excel in strength, that do his commandments, hearkening unto the voice of his word. Bless ye the LORD, all ye his hosts; ye ministers of his, that do his pleasure. Bless the LORD, all his works in all places of his dominion: bless the LORD, O my soul.*

Psalm 41:3—*The LORD will strengthen him upon the bed of languishing: thou wilt make all his bed in his sickness.*

John 16:20-22, NIV—*"Very truly I tell you, you will weep and mourn while the world rejoices. You will grieve, but your grief will turn to joy. A woman giving birth to a child has pain because her time has come; but when her baby is born she forgets the anguish because of her joy that a child is born into the world. So with you: Now is your time of grief, but I will see you again and you will rejoice, and no one will take away your joy."*

Psalm 30:2-3—*O Lord my God, I cried unto thee, and thou hast healed me. O Lord, thou hast brought up my soul from the grave: thou hast kept me alive, that I should not go down to the pit.*

Psalm 46:1—*God is our refuge and strength, a very present help in trouble.*

Psalm 10:9-13, NIV—*Like a lion in cover he lies in wait. He lies in wait to catch the helpless; he catches the helpless and drags them off in his net. His victims are crushed, they collapse; they fall under his strength. He says to himself, "God will never notice; he covers his face and never sees." Arise, Lord! Lift up your hand, O God. Do not forget the helpless. Why does the wicked man revile God? Why does he say to himself, "He won't call me to account"?*

Psalm 33:1-6—*Rejoice in the Lord, O ye righteous: for praise is comely for the upright. Praise the Lord with harp: sing unto him with the psaltery and an instrument of ten strings. Sing unto him a new song; play skilfully with a loud noise. For the word of the Lord is right; and all his works are done in truth. He loveth righteousness and judgment: the earth is full of the goodness of the Lord. By the word of the Lord were the heavens made; and all the host of them by the breath of his mouth.*

Psalm 90:1, NIV—*Lord, you have been our dwelling place throughout all generations.*

Psalm 91:1-4, NIV—*Whoever dwells in the shelter of the Most High will rest in the shadow of the Almighty. I will say of the* LORD, *"He is my refuge and my fortress, my God, in whom I trust." Surely he will save you from the fowler's snare and from the deadly pestilence. He will cover you with his feathers, and under his wings you will find refuge; his faithfulness will be your shield and rampart.*

Psalm 121:1-8—*I will lift up mine eyes unto the hills, from whence cometh my help. My help cometh from the* LORD, *which made heaven and earth. He will not suffer thy foot to be moved: he that keepeth thee will not slumber. Behold, he that keepeth Israel shall neither slumber nor sleep. The* LORD *is thy keeper: the* LORD *is thy shade upon thy right hand. The sun shall not smite thee by day, nor the moon by night. The* LORD *shall preserve thee from all evil: he shall preserve thy soul. The* LORD *shall preserve thy going out and thy coming in from this time forth, and even for evermore.*

Psalm 43:1-5, NIV—*Vindicate me, my God, and plead my cause against an unfaithful nation. Rescue me from those who are deceitful and wicked. You are God my stronghold. Why have you rejected me? Why must I go about mourning, oppressed by the enemy? Send me your light and your faithful care, let them lead me; let them bring me to your holy mountain, to the place where you dwell. Then I will go to the altar of God, to God, my joy and my delight. I will praise you with the lyre, O God, my God. Why, my soul, are you downcast? Why so disturbed within me? Put your hope in God, for I will yet praise him, my Savior and my God.*

Matthew 6:25-33—*Therefore I say unto you, Take no thought for your life, what ye shall eat, or what ye shall drink; nor yet for your body, what ye shall put on. Is not the life more than meat, and the body than raiment? Behold the fowls of the air: for they sow not, neither do they reap, nor gather into barns; yet your heavenly Father feedeth them. Are ye not much better than they? Which of you* *by taking thought can add one cubit unto his stature? And why take ye thought for raiment? Consider the lilies of the field, how they grow; they toil not, neither do they spin: and yet I say unto you, That even Solomon in all his glory was not arrayed like one of these. Wherefore, if God so clothe the grass of the field, which to day is, and to morrow is cast into the oven, shall he not much more clothe you, O ye of little faith? Therefore take no thought, saying, What shall we eat? or, What shall we drink? or, Wherewithal shall we be clothed? (For after all these things do the Gentiles seek:) for your heavenly Father knoweth that ye have need of all these things. But seek ye first the kingdom of God, and his righteousness; and all these things shall be added unto you.*

Matthew 7:7—*Ask, and it shall be given you; seek, and ye shall find; knock, and it shall be opened unto you.*

Matthew 11:28-30, NIV—*"Come to me, all you who are weary and burdened, and I will give you rest. Take my yoke upon you and learn from me, for I am gentle and humble in heart, and you will find rest for your souls. For my yoke is easy and my burden is light."*

John 14:1-3, NIV—*"Do not let your hearts be troubled. You believe in God; believe also in me. My Father's house has many rooms; if that were not so, would I have told you that I am going there to prepare a place for you? And if I go and prepare a place for you, I will come back and take you to be with me that you also may be where I am."*

Romans 8:35—*Who shall separate us from the love of Christ? shall tribulation, or distress, or persecution, or famine, or nakedness, or peril, or sword?*

Deuteronomy 7:15, NIV—*The L*ORD *will keep you free from every disease. He will not inflict on you the horrible diseases you knew in Egypt, but he will inflict them on all who hate you.*

Exodus 23:25, NIV—*"Worship the LORD your God, and his blessing will be on your food and water. I will take away sickness from among you."*

Psalm 34:19—*Many are the afflictions of the righteous: but the LORD delivereth him out of them all.*

Psalm 107:20—*He sent his word, and healed them, and delivered them from their destructions.*

Jeremiah 30:17, NIV—*"But I will restore you to health and heal your wounds, declares the LORD, because you are called an outcast, Zion for whom no one cares.'"*

Matthew 12:15, NIV—*Aware of this, Jesus withdrew from that place. A large crowd followed him, and he healed all who were ill.*

Matthew 14:14, NIV—*When Jesus landed and saw a large crowd, he had compassion on them and healed their sick.*

Comfort and Consolation

Psalm 34—*I will bless the LORD at all times: his praise shall continually be in my mouth. My soul shall make her boast in the LORD: the humble shall hear thereof, and be glad. O magnify the LORD with me, and let us exalt his name together. I sought the LORD, and he heard me, and delivered me from all my fears. They looked unto him, and were lightened: and their faces were not ashamed. This poor man cried, and the LORD heard him, and saved him out of all his troubles. The angel of the LORD encampeth round about them that fear him, and delivereth them. O taste and see that the LORD is good: blessed is the man that trusteth in him. O fear the LORD, ye his saints: for there is no want to them that fear him. The young lions do lack, and suffer hunger: but they that seek the LORD shall not want any good thing. Come, ye children, hearken unto* *me: I will teach you the fear of the* LORD. *What man is he that desireth life, and loveth many days, that he may see good? Keep thy tongue from evil, and thy lips from speaking guile. Depart from evil, and do good; seek peace, and pursue it. The eyes of the* LORD *are upon the righteous, and his ears are open unto their cry. The face of the* LORD *is against them that do evil, to cut off the remembrance of them from the earth. The righteous cry, and the* LORD *heareth, and delivereth them out of all their troubles. The* LORD *is nigh unto them that are of a broken heart; and saveth such as be of a contrite spirit. Many are the afflictions of the righteous: but the* LORD *delivereth him out of them all.*

Psalm 91:1, NIV—*Whoever dwells in the shelter of the Most High will rest in the shadow of the Almighty.*

Isaiah 63:7-9, NIV—*I will tell of the kindnesses of the* LORD, *the deeds for which he is to be praised, according to all the* LORD *has done for us—yes, the many good things he has done for Israel, according to his compassion and many kindnesses. He said, "Surely they are my people, children who will be true to me"; and so he became their Savior. In all their distress he too was distressed, and the angel of his presence saved them. In his love and mercy he redeemed them; he lifted them up and carried them all the days of old.*

Isaiah 40—*Comfort ye, comfort ye my people, saith your God. Speak ye comfortably to Jerusalem, and cry unto her, that her warfare is accomplished, that her iniquity is pardoned: for she hath received of the* LORD*'s hand double for all her sins. The voice of him that crieth in the wilderness, Prepare ye the way of the* LORD, *make straight in the desert a highway for our God. Every valley shall be exalted, and every mountain and hill shall be made low: and the crooked shall be made straight, and the rough places plain: and the glory of the* LORD *shall be revealed, and all flesh shall see it together: for the mouth of the* LORD *hath spoken it. The voice said, Cry. And he said, What shall I cry? All flesh is grass, and all the goodliness thereof is as the flower of the field: the* *grass withereth, the flower fadeth: because the spirit of the* LORD *bloweth upon it: surely the people is grass. The grass withereth, the flower fadeth: but the word of our God shall stand for ever. O Zion, that bringest good tidings, get thee up into the high mountain; O Jerusalem, that bringest good tidings, lift up thy voice with strength; lift it up, be not afraid; say unto the cities of Judah, Behold your God! Behold, the Lord* GOD *will come with strong hand, and his arm shall rule for him: behold, his reward is with him, and his work before him. He shall feed his flock like a shepherd: he shall gather the lambs with his arm, and carry them in his bosom, and shall gently lead those that are with young.*

Romans 8:18-28—*For I reckon that the sufferings of this present time are not worthy to be compared with the glory which shall be revealed in us. For the earnest expectation of the creature waiteth for the manifestation of the sons of God. For the creature was made subject to vanity, not willingly, but by reason of him who hath subjected the same in hope, because the creature itself also shall be delivered from the bondage of corruption into the glorious liberty of the children of God. For we know that the whole creation groaneth and travaileth in pain together until now. And not only they, but ourselves also, which have the firstfruits of the Spirit, even we ourselves groan within ourselves, waiting for the adoption, to wit, the redemption of our body. For we are saved by hope: but hope that is seen is not hope: for what a man seeth, why doth he yet hope for? But if we hope for that we see not, then do we with patience wait for it. Likewise the Spirit also helpeth our infirmities: for we know not what we should pray for as we ought: but the Spirit itself maketh intercession for us with groanings which cannot be uttered. And he that searcheth the hearts knoweth what is the mind of the Spirit, because he maketh intercession for the saints according to the will of God. And we know that all things work together for good to them that love God, to them who are the called according to his purpose.*

1 Thessalonians 5:1-11, NIV—*Now, brothers and sisters, about times and dates we do not need to write to you, for you know very well that the day of the Lord will come like a thief in the night. While people are saying, "Peace and safety," destruction will come on them suddenly, as labor pains on a pregnant woman, and they will not escape. But you, brothers and sisters, are not in darkness so that this day should surprise you like a thief. You are all children of the light and children of the day. We do not belong to the night or to the darkness. So then, let us not be like others, who are asleep, but let us be awake and sober. For those who sleep, sleep at night, and those who get drunk, get drunk at night. But since we belong to the day, let us be sober, putting on faith and love as a breastplate, and the hope of salvation as a helmet. For God did not appoint us to suffer wrath but to receive salvation through our Lord Jesus Christ. He died for us so that, whether we are awake or asleep, we may live together with him. Therefore encourage one another and build each other up, just as in fact you are doing.*

1 Peter 2:11-12—*Dearly beloved, I beseech you as strangers and pilgrims, abstain from fleshly lusts, which war against the soul; having your conversation honest among the Gentiles: that, whereas they speak against you as evildoers, they may by your good works, which they shall behold, glorify God in the day of visitation.*

1 Peter 2:19-25, NIV—*For it is commendable if someone bears up under the pain of unjust suffering because they are conscious of God. But how is it to your credit if you receive a beating for doing wrong and endure it? But if you suffer for doing good and you endure it, this is commendable before God. To this you were called, because Christ suffered for you, leaving you an example, that you should follow in his steps. "He committed no sin, and no deceit was found in his mouth." When they hurled their insults at him, he did not retaliate; when he suffered, he made no threats. Instead, he entrusted himself to him who judges justly. "He himself bore our sins" in his body on the cross, so that* we might die to sins and live for righteousness; "by his wounds you have been healed." For "you were like sheep going astray," but now you have returned to the Shepherd and Overseer of your souls.

After the Burial

John 3:16—*For God so loved the world, that he gave his only begotten Son, that whosoever believeth in him should not perish, but have everlasting life.*

Psalm 23:4—*Yea, though I walk through the valley of the shadow of death, I will fear no evil: for thou art with me; thy rod and thy staff they comfort me.*

Psalm 27:1—*The LORD is my light and my salvation; whom shall I fear? the LORD is the strength of my life; of whom shall I be afraid?*

Romans 8:14-39—*For as many as are led by the Spirit of God, they are the sons of God. For ye have not received the spirit of bondage again to fear; but ye have received the Spirit of adoption, whereby we cry, Abba, Father. The Spirit itself beareth witness with our spirit, that we are the children of God: and if children, then heirs; heirs of God, and joint-heirs with Christ; if so be that we suffer with him, that we may be also glorified together. For I reckon that the sufferings of this present time are not worthy to be compared with the glory which shall be revealed in us. For the earnest expectation of the creature waiteth for the manifestation of the sons of God. For the creature was made subject to vanity, not willingly, but by reason of him who hath subjected the same in hope, because the creature itself also shall be delivered from the bondage of corruption into the glorious liberty of the children of God. For we know that the whole creation groaneth and travaileth in pain together until now. And not only they, but ourselves also, which have the firstfruits of the Spirit, even we ourselves groan within ourselves, waiting for the adoption, to wit, the redemption of our body. For we are saved by hope: but hope that is seen is not* *hope: for what a man seeth, why doth he yet hope for? But if we hope for that we see not, then do we with patience wait for it. Likewise the Spirit also helpeth our infirmities: for we know not what we should pray for as we ought: but the Spirit itself maketh intercession for us with groanings which cannot be uttered. And he that searcheth the hearts knoweth what is the mind of the Spirit, because he maketh intercession for the saints according to the will of God. And we know that all things work together for good to them that love God, to them who are the called according to his purpose. For whom he did foreknow, he also did predestinate to be conformed to the image of his Son, that he might be the firstborn among many brethren. Moreover whom he did predestinate, them he also called: and whom he called, them he also justified: and whom he justified, them he also glorified. What shall we then say to these things? If God be for us, who can be against us? He that spared not his own Son, but delivered him up for us all, how shall he not with him also freely give us all things? Who shall lay any thing to the charge of God's elect? It is God that justifieth. Who is he that condemneth? It is Christ that died, yea rather, that is risen again, who is even at the right hand of God, who also maketh intercession for us. Who shall separate us from the love of Christ? shall tribulation, or distress, or persecution, or famine, or nakedness, or peril, or sword? As it is written, For thy sake we are killed all the day long; we are accounted as sheep for the slaughter. Nay, in all these things we are more than conquerors through him that loved us. For I am persuaded, that neither death, nor life, nor angels, nor principalities, nor powers, nor things present, nor things to come, nor height, nor depth, nor any other creature, shall be able to separate us from the love of God, which is in Christ Jesus our Lord.*

Revelation 21:1-4—*And I saw a new heaven and a new earth: for the first heaven and the first earth were passed away; and there was no more sea. And I John saw the holy city, new Jerusalem, coming down from God out of heaven, prepared as a bride adorned for her husband. And I heard a great voice out of heaven saying, Behold, the tabernacle of God is with men, and he will dwell with them, and they shall be his people, and God himself shall be with them,* and be their God. And God shall wipe away all tears from their eyes; and there shall be no more death, neither sorrow, nor crying, neither shall there be any more pain: for the former things are passed away.

Revelation 21:22-26—*And I saw no temple therein: for the Lord God Almighty and the Lamb are the temple of it. And the city had no need of the sun, neither of the moon, to shine in it: for the glory of God did lighten it, and the Lamb is the light thereof. And the nations of them which are saved shall walk in the light of it: and the kings of the earth do bring their glory and honour into it. And the gates of it shall not be shut at all by day: for there shall be no night there. And they shall bring the glory and honour of the nations into it.*

The Resurrection

John 11:11-26, NIV—*After he had said this, he went on to tell them, "Our friend Lazarus has fallen asleep; but I am going there to wake him up." His disciples replied, "Lord, if he sleeps, he will get better." Jesus had been speaking of his death, but his disciples thought he meant natural sleep. So then he told them plainly, "Lazarus is dead, and for your sake I am glad I was not there, so that you may believe. But let us go to him." Then Thomas (also known as Didymus) said to the rest of the disciples, "Let us also go, that we may die with him." On his arrival, Jesus found that Lazarus had already been in the tomb for four days. Now Bethany was less than two miles from Jerusalem, and many Jews had come to Martha and Mary to comfort them in the loss of their brother. When Martha heard that Jesus was coming, she went out to meet him, but Mary stayed at home. "Lord," Martha said to Jesus, "if you had been here, my brother would not have died. But I know that even now God will give you whatever you ask." Jesus said to her, "Your brother will rise again." Martha answered, "I know he will rise again in the resurrection at the last day." Jesus said to her, "I am the resurrection and the life. The one who believes in me will live, even though they die; and whoever lives by believing in me will never die. Do you believe this?"*

John 20:1-18, NIV—*Early on the first day of the week, while it was still dark, Mary Magdalene went to the tomb and saw that the stone had been removed from the entrance. So she came running to Simon Peter and the other disciple, the one Jesus loved, and said, "They have taken the Lord out of the tomb, and we don't know where they have put him!" So Peter and the other disciple started for the tomb. Both were running, but the other disciple outran Peter and reached the tomb first. He bent over and looked in at the strips of linen lying there but did not go in. Then Simon Peter came along behind him and went straight into the tomb. He saw the strips of linen lying there, as well as the cloth that had been wrapped around Jesus' head. The cloth was still lying in its place, separate from the linen. Finally the other disciple, who had reached the tomb first, also went inside. He saw and believed. (They still did not understand from Scripture that Jesus had to rise from the dead.) Then the disciples went back to where they were staying. Now Mary stood outside the tomb crying. As she wept, she bent over to look into the tomb and saw two angels in white, seated where Jesus' body had been, one at the head and the other at the foot. They asked her, "Woman, why are you crying?" "They have taken my Lord away," she said, "and I don't know where they have put him." At this, she turned around and saw Jesus standing there, but she did not realize that it was Jesus. He asked her, "Woman, why are you crying? Who is it you are looking for?" Thinking he was the gardener, she said, "Sir, if you have carried him away, tell me where you have put him, and I will get him." Jesus said to her, "Mary." She turned toward him and cried out in Aramaic, "Rabboni!" (which means "Teacher"). Jesus said, "Do not hold on to me, for I have not yet ascended to the Father. Go instead to my brothers and tell them, 'I am ascending to my Father and your Father, to my God and your God.'" Mary Magdalene went to the disciples with the news: "I have seen the Lord!" And she told them that he had said these things to her.*

1 Corinthians 15:20-24—*But now is Christ risen from the dead, and become the firstfruits of them that slept. For since by man came death, by* man came also the resurrection of the dead. For as in Adam all die, even so in Christ shall all be made alive. But every man in his own order: Christ the firstfruits; afterward they that are Christ's at his coming. Then cometh the end, when he shall have delivered up the kingdom to God, even the Father; when he shall have put down all rule and all authority and power.

1 Corinthians 15:29-32—*Else what shall they do which are baptized for the dead, if the dead rise not at all? why are they then baptized for the dead? And why stand we in jeopardy every hour? I protest by your rejoicing which I have in Christ Jesus our Lord, I die daily. If after the manner of men I have fought with beasts at Ephesus, what advantageth it me, if the dead rise not? let us eat and drink; for to morrow we die.*

1 Corinthians 15:35-50, NIV—*But someone will ask, "How are the dead raised? With what kind of body will they come?" How foolish! What you sow does not come to life unless it dies. When you sow, you do not plant the body that will be, but just a seed, perhaps of wheat or of something else. But God gives it a body as he has determined, and to each kind of seed he gives its own body. Not all flesh is the same: People have one kind of flesh, animals have another, birds another and fish another. There are also heavenly bodies and there are earthly bodies; but the splendor of the heavenly bodies is one kind, and the splendor of the earthly bodies is another. The sun has one kind of splendor, the moon another and the stars another; and star differs from star in splendor. So will it be with the resurrection of the dead. The body that is sown is perishable, it is raised imperishable; it is sown in dishonor, it is raised in glory; it is sown in weakness, it is raised in power; it is sown a natural body, it is raised a spiritual body. If there is a natural body, there is also a spiritual body. So it is written: "The first man Adam became a living being"; the last Adam, a life-giving spirit. The spiritual did not come first, but the natural, and after that the spiritual. The first man was of the dust of the earth; the second man is of heaven. As was the earthly man, so are those who are of the earth;*

and as is the heavenly man, so also are those who are of heaven. And just as we have borne the image of the earthly man, so shall we bear the image of the heavenly man. I declare to you, brothers and sisters, that flesh and blood cannot inherit the kingdom of God, nor does the perishable inherit the imperishable.

How to Overcome the Fear of Death

John 14:1-7—*Let not your heart be troubled: ye believe in God, believe also in me. In my Father's house are many mansions: if it were not so, I would have told you. I go to prepare a place for you. And if I go and prepare a place for you, I will come again, and receive you unto myself; that where I am, there ye may be also. And whither I go ye know, and the way ye know. Thomas saith unto him, Lord, we know not whither thou goest; and how can we know the way? Jesus saith unto him, I am the way, the truth, and the life: no man cometh unto the Father, but by me. If ye had known me, ye should have known my Father also: and from henceforth ye know him, and have seen him.*

Hebrews 2:14-15—*Forasmuch then as the children are partakers of flesh and blood, he also himself likewise took part of the same; that through death he might destroy him that had the power of death, that is, the devil; and deliver them who through fear of death were all their lifetime subject to bondage.*

Hebrews 7:9-17—*And as I may so say, Levi also, who receiveth tithes, payed tithes in Abraham. For he was yet in the loins of his father, when Melchisedec met him. If therefore perfection were by the Levitical priesthood, (for under it the people received the law,) what further need was there that another priest should rise after the order of Melchisedec, and not be called after the order of Aaron? For the priesthood being changed, there is made of necessity a change also of the law. For he of whom these things are spoken pertaineth to another tribe, of which no man gave attendance at the altar. For it is evident that our Lord sprang out of Juda; of which tribe Moses spake nothing* concerning priesthood. And it is yet far more evident: for that after the similitude of Melchisedec there ariseth another priest, who is made, not after the law of a carnal commandment, but after the power of an endless life. For he testifieth, Thou art a priest for ever after the order of Melchisedec.

Sudden or Accidental Death

Job 21:13, NIV—*"They spend their years in prosperity and go down to the grave in peace."*

Proverbs 27:1, NIV—*Do not boast about tomorrow, for you do not know what a day may bring.*

Matthew 24:42, NIV—*"Therefore keep watch, because you do not know on what day your Lord will come."*

1 Thessalonians 5:2—*For yourselves know perfectly that the day of the Lord so cometh as a thief in the night.*

1 Thessalonians 5:6—*Therefore let us not sleep, as do others; but let us watch and be sober.*

James 4:14, NIV—*Why, you do not even know what will happen tomorrow. What is your life? You are a mist that appears for a little while and then vanishes.*

The Death of a Parent

Genesis 50:1-13—*And Joseph fell upon his father's face, and wept upon him, and kissed him. And Joseph commanded his servants the physicians to embalm his father: and the physicians embalmed Israel. And forty days were fulfilled for him; for so are fulfilled the days of those which are embalmed: and the*

Egyptians mourned for him threescore and ten days. And when the days of his mourning were past, Joseph spake unto the house of Pharaoh, saying, If now I have found grace in your eyes, speak, I pray you, in the ears of Pharaoh, saying, My father made me swear, saying, Lo, I die: in my grave which I have digged for me in the land of Canaan, there shalt thou bury me. Now therefore let me go up, I pray thee, and bury my father, and I will come again. And Pharaoh said, Go up, and bury thy father, according as he made thee swear. And Joseph went up to bury his father: and with him went up all the servants of Pharaoh, the elders of his house, and all the elders of the land of Egypt, and all the house of Joseph, and his brethren, and his father's house: only their little ones, and their flocks, and their herds, they left in the land of Goshen. And there went up with him both chariots and horsemen: and it was a very great company. And they came to the threshingfloor of Atad, which is beyond Jordan, and there they mourned with a great and very sore lamentation: and he made a mourning for his father seven days. And when the inhabitants of the land, the Canaanites, saw the mourning in the floor of Atad, they said, This is a grievous mourning to the Egyptians: wherefore the name of it was called Abelmizraim, which is beyond Jordan. And his sons did unto him according as he commanded them: for his sons carried him into the land of Canaan, and buried him in the cave of the field of Machpelah, which Abraham bought with the field for a possession of a buryingplace of Ephron the Hittite, before Mamre.

Psalm 27:10—*When my father and my mother forsake me, then the* LORD *will take me up.*

Psalm 35:14—*I behaved myself as though he had been my friend or brother: I bowed down heavily, as one that mourneth for his mother.*

Psalm 68:5, NIV—*A father to the fatherless, a defender of widows, is God in his holy dwelling.*

Proverbs 20:7—*The just man walketh in his integrity: his children are blessed after him.*

Death in the Prime of Life

Genesis 11:28, NIV—*While his father Terah was still alive, Haran died in Ur of the Chaldeans, in the land of his birth.*

Job 21:23, NIV—*One person dies in full vigor, completely secure and at ease.*

Jeremiah 15:9, NIV—*"The mother of seven will grow faint and breathe her last. Her sun will set while it is still day; she will be disgraced and humiliated. I will put the survivors to the sword before their enemies," declares the* LORD.

Jeremiah 48:17, NIV—*"Mourn for her, all who live around her, all who know her fame; say, 'How broken is the mighty scepter, how broken the glorious staff!'"*

Luke 14:30—*This man began to build, and was not able to finish.*

The Death of the Aged

Genesis 15:15—*And thou shalt go to thy fathers in peace; thou shalt be buried in a good old age.*

Genesis 25:8—*Then Abraham gave up the ghost, and died in a good old age, an old man, and full of years; and was gathered to his people.*

Genesis 27:2, NIV—*Isaac said, "I am now an old man and don't know the day of my death."*

Job 5:26, NIV—*You will come to the grave in full vigor, like sheaves gathered in season.*

Psalm 91:16—*With long life will I satisfy him, and shew him my salvation.*

Zechariah 14:7, NIV—*It will be a unique day—a day known only to the* LORD—*with no distinction between day and night. When evening comes, there will be light.*

The Death of a Child

1 Samuel 1:28, NIV—*"So now I give him to the* LORD. *For his whole life he will be given over to the* LORD.*" And he worshiped the* LORD *there.*

2 Samuel 12:16-23—*David therefore besought God for the child; and David fasted, and went in, and lay all night upon the earth. And the elders of his house arose, and went to him, to raise him up from the earth: but he would not, neither did he eat bread with them. And it came to pass on the seventh day, that the child died. And the servants of David feared to tell him that the child was dead: for they said, Behold, while the child was yet alive, we spake unto him, and he would not hearken unto our voice: how will he then vex himself, if we tell him that the child is dead? But when David saw that his servants whispered, David perceived that the child was dead: therefore David said unto his servants, Is the child dead? And they said, He is dead. Then David arose from the earth, and washed, and anointed himself, and changed his apparel, and came into the house of the* LORD, *and worshipped: then he came to his own house; and when he required, they set bread before him, and he did eat. Then said his servants unto him, What thing is this that thou hast done? thou didst fast and weep for the child, while it was alive; but when the child was dead, thou didst rise and eat bread. And he said, While the child was yet alive, I fasted and wept: for I said, Who can tell whether God will be gracious to me, that the* *child may live? But now he is dead, wherefore should I fast? can I bring him back again? I shall go to him, but he shall not return to me.*

Job 1:21—*Naked came I out of my mother's womb, and naked shall I return thither: the LORD gave, and the LORD hath taken away; blessed be the name of the LORD.*

Isaiah 11:6—*The wolf also shall dwell with the lamb, and the leopard shall lie down with the kid; and the calf and the young lion and the fatling together; and a little child shall lead them.*

Matthew 18:1-6—*At the same time came the disciples unto Jesus, saying, Who is the greatest in the kingdom of heaven? And Jesus called a little child unto him, and set him in the midst of them, and said, Verily I say unto you, Except ye be converted, and become as little children, ye shall not enter into the kingdom of heaven. Whosoever therefore shall humble himself as this little child, the same is greatest in the kingdom of heaven. And whoso shall receive one such little child in my name receiveth me. But whoso shall offend one of these little ones which believe in me, it were better for him that a millstone were hanged about his neck, and that he were drowned in the depth of the sea.*

Matthew 19:14, NIV—*Jesus said, "Let the little children come to me, and do not hinder them, for the kingdom of heaven belongs to such as these."*

Mark 10:13-16—*And they brought young children to him, that he should touch them: and his disciples rebuked those that brought them. But when Jesus saw it, he was much displeased, and said unto them, Suffer the little children to come unto me, and forbid them not: for of such is the kingdom of God. Verily I say unto you, Whosoever shall not receive the kingdom of God as a little child, he shall not enter therein. And he took them up in his arms, put his hands upon them, and blessed them.*

Bibliography

Becker, Arthur. *The Compassionate Visitor: Resources for Ministering to People Who Are Ill*. Minneapolis: Fortress Press, 1985.

"End-of-Life Care Decisions." bannerhealth.com. http://www.bannerhealth.com/patients/advance-directives/decisions (accessed October 20, 2017).

Ford, Michael. *Wounded Prophet*. New York: Doubleday, 2002.

Hope for the Heart. "Terminal Illness." Quick Reference Counseling Keys Excerpt. http://www.hopefortheheart.org/pdfs/OLQR-pr-Terminal%20Illness.pdf.

Hunt, Roger. "Yes, Lord; I Believe that You Are the Christ." Orthodox Christian Network, April 22, 2016. http://myocn.net/yes-lord-i-believe-that-you-are-the-christ/

Johnson, Darrell W. "Biblical Requirements of Leaders." *Christianity Today*, July 2007. http://www.christianitytoday.com/pastors/2007/july-online-only/le-040329.html.

Jongsma, Arthur E., Jr., and Frank M. Dattilio. *The Family Therapy Treatment Planner*. New York: John Wiley & Sons, 2000.

Kelcourse, Felicity. "P-500: Basics of Pastoral Care & Counseling." Course description. Indianapolis, IN: Christian Theological Seminary, Spring 2012.

Kok, James R., and Arthur E. Jongsma Jr. *The Pastoral Counseling Treatment Planner*. New York: John Wiley & Sons, 1998.

Kolf, June Cerza. *When Will I Stop Hurting?: Dealing with a Recent Death*. Grand Rapids, MI: Baker Books, 2002.

Kübler-Ross, Elizabeth. *On Death and Dying*, 1st ed. New York: Macmillan Company, 1969.

McKiddie, Eric. "3 Simple Steps to an Encouraging Hospital Visit." *Pastoralized*, July 30, 2012. http://www.pastoralized.com/2012/07/30/3-simple-steps-to-an-encouraging-hospital-visit/.

Moore, Bret A., and Arthur E. Jongsma Jr. *The Veterans and Active Duty Military Psychotherapy Treatment Planner*. New York: John Wiley & Sons, 2009.

"My Working Definition of Pastoral Care." *Journeying Alongside* (January 2012). Retrieved from https://journeyingalongside.wordpress.com/2012/01/20/my-working-definition-of-pastoral-care/.

Nouwen, Henri, *Creative Ministry.* New York: Image Doubleday, 1971.

———. *The Wounded Healer.* New York: Image Doubleday, 2010.

Perkinson, Robert R., and Arthur E. Jongsma Jr. T*he Chemical Dependence Treatment Planner.* New York: John Wiley & Sons, 1998.

Remen, Rachel Naomi. "Helping, Fixing, or Serving," *Awaken.org*, May 2000. http://www.awaken.org.

Schultheis, Gary, Steffanie O'Hanlon, and Bill O'Hanlon. *Couples Therapy Homework Planner*, 2nd ed. Series editor Arthur E. Jongsma Jr. New York: John Wiley & Sons, 2010.

Shelly, Bruce L. "7 Essentials of a Healthy Hospital Visit." *Christianity Today Leadership Journal* (August 2012). http://www.christianitytoday.com/le/2012/august-online-only/healthy-hospital-visit.html.

Singh, Kathleen Dowling. "Taking a Spiritual Inventory." National Caregivers Library. http://www.caregiverslibrary.org/caregivers-resources/grp-end-of-life-issues/taking-a-spiritual-inventory-article.aspx.

Williams, Emmanuel L. "Effective Hospital Visitation." *Enrichment Journal.* http://enrichmentjournal.ag.org/200403/200403_112_hospitalvisitation.cfm (accessed October 16, 2017).

Wimberly, Edward. *African American Pastoral Care*, revised edition. Nashville: Abingdon Press, 2010.

Wolfelt, Alan D. "Understanding Common Patterns of Avoiding Grief." *Interpersonal Skills Training: A Handbook for Funeral Service Staffs.* http://www.idhca.org/wp-content/uploads/2017/07/Hiles_Understanding-Common-Patterns-of-Grief-Avoidance.pdf.

Woolley, Douglas E. "Pastoral Care on the New Testament Epistles." Harrison School of Graduate Studies, Southwestern Assemblies of God University, Waxahachie, TX, 2009.

Wooten, Thomas J. *Seasoned with Salt: Seasoned for the Day of Redemption.* North Charleston, SC: CreateSpace Independent Publishing, 2015.

Zoba, Wendy Murray. "Dying in Peace." *Christianity Today*, October 2001. http://www.christianitytoday.com/ct/2001/october22/9.80.html.

Biographical Sketch for Reverend Dr. Nevalon Mitchell Jr.

 Born in Wilson, North Carolina, Dr. Nevalon Mitchell Jr. has more than thirty-five years of experience as a minister, counselor, and instructor. He is president/owner of Nevalon Mitchell Jr. Ministries Inc. and Life Enrichment Counseling and Support Services LLC. He also is staff chaplain for the Department of Veterans Affairs Medical Healthcare System in Baltimore, Maryland.

Dr. Mitchell holds dual membership as a board-certified expert in both the National Center for Crisis Management and the National Center for Traumatic Stress. He holds addiction counselor certifications in Colorado, Maryland, and Washington, DC. He is a marriage and family therapy license candidate in Colorado.

He served as a chaplain in the United States Army, retiring in July 2000 as a lieutenant colonel. He holds a life membership with the Disabled American Veterans, the American Legion, and the Veterans of Foreign Wars of the United States.

He holds a Bachelor of Arts degree in sociology, a minor in psychology, and a basic intensive in philosophy from the University of Michigan in Flint. He also has a Master of Divinity degree from Garrett-Evangelical Theological Seminary, and a Doctor of Ministry degree from the Louisville Presbyterian Theological Seminary. He also has a PhD in church history and biblical studies from Newburgh Theological Seminary.

Dr. Mitchell is a licensed and ordained minister in the National Baptist Convention, USA, Inc. He was selected by the 2003, 2008, and 2012 National Baptist Congress of Christian Education, National Baptist Convention, USA, Inc., as an instructor in the Ministers' Division. Dr. Mitchell introduced the first class on post-traumatic stress disorder to the National Baptist Convention in Detroit, Michigan, in 2003. He also served as an instructor in the National Capital Congress of Christian Education and a certified instructor in the United Baptist Missionary Congress of Christian Education, United Baptist Missionary Convention of Maryland, 2006–2008.

His professional affiliations include the American Psychotherapy Association, the Association of Mental Health Clergy, the Association for Clinical Pastoral Education, the American Association of Pastoral Counselors, the American Counseling Association, the National Association of Alcoholism and Drug Abuse Counselors, the Department of Veterans Affairs National Black Chaplains Association, and the National Association of Veterans Affairs Chaplains (NAVAC). Dr. Mitchell is considered by NAVAC as the resident expert with a Specialty Certification in Substance Abuse. He is also a clinical member of the Association of Professional Chaplains.

He has conducted many workshops and seminars. He also has written and cowritten numerous articles and books. His recently released book is entitled *The Liberation of the Black Church and the Preacher: Overcoming Tradition through Kingdom Principles.*

He and his wife, Wessylyne Kaye, are the proud parents of three adult children, seven adorable grandchildren, and two godchildren. Dr. Mitchell is a member of Kappa Alpha Psi Fraternity, Inc.

www.ingramcontent.com/pod-product-compliance
Lightning Source LLC
Chambersburg PA
CBHW071531080526
44588CB00011B/1637